planning the perfect

perfect

Acknowledgements

Published by
Kensington West Productions,
5 Cattle Market, Hexham, Northumberland NE46 1NJ
Tel: (01434) 609933 Fax: (01434) 600066
E mail: kwp@kensingtonwest.demon.co.uk

in association with
Elegant Days,
The Lodge, Hatton House, Hatton, Warwickshire CV35 7LD
Tel: (01926) 842044 Fax: (01926) 843381

Editor:
Silver Sheldon

Sub Editors:
Shelagh Martell, Helen Parker, Karen Ryan

Production:
Mark Scandle

Design:
Diane Ridley, Nick Ridley

Origination by:
Pre-Press Ltd, Hong Kong

Printed by:
Liang Yu Printing Factory Ltd, Hong Kong

courtesy of Pains Fireworks

Introduction

I am delighted to introduce the first edition of Planning the Perfect Party. Elegant Days has been at the forefront of Corporate Party Planning for fifteen years and has been voted Event Manager Of The Year for the last two years. We and our colleagues are delighted to have this opportunity to pass on some valuable insights into Planning the Perfect Party.

As the start of the third millennium approaches, we anticipate many great party opportunities. We can celebrate the millennium, old and new, the century, old and new, and what better way to do it than to party? Parties offer unlimited scope for celebration, expression and participation and we hope the following pages inspire you to join the party.

One word of warning. The very fact that parties offer unlimited scope for expression and enjoyment also means there is enormous scope for the old adage "what can go wrong will go wrong" to come into play. To keep mishaps to a minimum, plan with care, employ professionals and invite wisely. We know the perfect party is Utopia, but we hope these few insights will go some way towards ensuring your own celebrations are counted among next year's Perfect Parties.

Eddie Hoare
Managing Director, Elegant Days Ltd

Elegant Days Ltd, Event Manager of the Year 1996 & 1997
Tel: (01926) 842044 Fax: (01926) 843381

courtesy of Searcy's

Contents

Contents

Chapter 5 Under Cover

Chapter 6 At Home

Chapter 7 Location, location, location

Chapter 8 Contributors

courtesy of The Banqueting House, Whitehall Palace

Le vin c'est pas nécessaire
Mais Dieu ne le défend pas
Il eût créé la vigne amère
S'il eût voula qu'on en but pas

party
Party.
party
Party

party

party

Party !

Much of the fun is in the planning, but not for everybody. There are some people who simply love organising and to these people planning a party is nirvana. A party, like life, can be as complicated as you make it and as in life, it is often the most straightforward simple things that cause the most anxiety.

The simplest type of party I've ever been involved with was the setting up of a beach bar. It happened nightly for three weeks until an over-zealous official put a stop to it (we hadn't let her in on the idea - big mistake) and while it worked, it worked gloriously. The bar was made up of two wind surfers, food was bought the same day - simple fare - pâté, cheese and French sticks and the booze was a momentous punch made from everything and anything - lethal! Guests paid a flat fee of £5 and they all went away content. That was nearly twenty years ago but the value was superb. The other option was to have an expensive drink in one of the exclusive French bars - two cocktails if you were lucky! And so it was, by offering atmosphere and value, we arrived at a simple formula and every evening was a winner.

In this book there are numerous ideas given by professionals in their trade - from lighting to flowers, from fireworks to furniture. Many of the ideas are simple but if you follow them, then with hard work and some luck your party will be a corker. It might not be perfect - what party ever is? - but it will be fun and that's what matters.

Why do people party?

I was once told by my uncle Gervaise that if ever you require an answer to a particularly troublesome question, you should ask a child. Children invariably get straight to the point, unburdened by the complexities of grown-up life. So, when presented with that hoary chestnut "Why do people party?", I turned in desperation to my five year old daughter.

"Why do people party?" I asked.

"For the presents of course. Don't you know anything?"

And when I thought about it I realised she was right. People party with the expectation that they will get something in return. OK, so the Chairman of Megacorp plc doesn't expect to receive a Ken and Barbie dressing up kit or a Little Mermaid make-up set just because he puts on a corporate thrash at The Savoy, but on the other hand he hasn't invited his guests out of the goodness of his heart, now has he? Similarly, the mother who throws herself body and soul into the organisation of her daughter's wedding may convince herself that it's all for the girl's benefit, but she's not fooling anyone else. This is mum's big chance to blow the family trumpet and show off her new frock.

So, the guests, the people who go to the party, expect something in return for giving up their valuable time and undoubted wit. My daughter expects a party bag (a curse on whoever came up with that idea), but the majority of partygoers expect to be entertained, fed and watered and to be given the opportunity to mix, network and show themselves off. Not much to ask, is it?

When we were young, free and single (and a bit spotty, should the truth be known) we went to parties for one thing and one thing only. Never got it of course, but that didn't stop us from going to more parties.

Maybe there is no such thing as the wholly altruistic party - everybody is in it for something. The cup of history overflows with examples of some pretty spectacular thrashes designed to further the interests of the participants. When Henry VIII received his invitation to the Field of the Cloth of Gold he knew exactly what Francis I was after; but he went anyway, had a great time and then said "No". Now there's a party animal for you! Lesson One: Lavish spreads don't necessarily guarantee lavish results.

courtesy of Joanna Plumbe photography

A GOOD EXCUSE

Given that every party carries with it some ulterior motive, innocent as it may be, you still need an excuse to push the boat out. Even the Mad Hatter had to come up with the Unbirthday Party.

For family and friends the excuse is usually a rite of passage. Some rites of passage are more popular than others. The ones at the beginning and the end - Christenings and Funerals - should be avoided like the plague. Christenings invariably revolve around potted meat sandwiches (where do they find it?), lukewarm Darjeeling, sickly cake, half a glass of sweet Bulgarian fizz and some devastatingly dull speeches. Funerals, on the other hand, can be quite jolly affairs: people are far more friendly, there are no speeches and the drink seldom runs out. These are not really the sort of events that most hosts plan for with great alacrity, however.

This leaves us with "The Coming of Age" party, "The Wedding", "The Big Birthday" (usually anything with a zero in it) and of course "The Wedding Anniversary". In every case we are supposed to be partying in recognition of an important phase in an individual's life, but, let's face it, we've really just come up with another excuse to let our hair down - if we've got any left that is.

New Year's Eve is also a pretty fine excuse for a knees-up, but you can only do it properly if you have a legitimate reason to wear a kilt and can sing "Auld Lang Syne" comfortably with your head shoved up the armpit of a drunken docker from Greenock. Personally, I would leave Hogmanay to the Scots. We Sassenachs usually end up getting maudlin about the past year whilst swearing eternal friendship to a group of strangers we'll never meet again.

Companies, on the other hand, have to find different excuses to party and have far more cavalier reasons for doing so: Christmas, anniversaries, annual awards and sports hospitality are the staples of the corporate host and in every case the parties are designed to oil the wheels of commerce. Whether it's to reward staff for their endeavours and motivate them for the future or to rub shoulders with clients outside the normal working environment, the corporate party always has to be justified by the bottom line.

courtesy of The Ice Box

A GOOD MIX

Once you've found a decent enough excuse to push the boat out, there's the almost insurmountable problem of the guest list. For a party to succeed you need the right mix of people. The sort of good eggs who like to have a good time and enjoy having it with other people. Unfortunately, no matter what the occasion, private or corporate, you will never have the luxury of inviting only those guests you want. You will also have to consider the "Must Asks".

"Must Asks" come in four varieties according to the type of party you are organising. These are: the unavoidable relative, the unwanted friend, the unignorable client and the insufferable colleague.

Unavoidable relatives include the likes of Great Aunt Maud who hasn't smiled since the Relief of Mafeking (senna apparently) or Cousin Angus who is so certain of his own ability that he could tell Richard Branson a thing or two about running a successful company and would explain the finer points of the cross-court-pass to Pete Sampras given half a chance.

The unwanted friend is either a chum from way back at junior school with halitosis who won't disappear and still calls you "Tubby", or the spouse of a good friend who can't understand what your good friend saw in you in the first place.

The corporate host is dealt a far harsher hand when it comes to the "Must Asks", as there is the bottom line to think of. There is always the leering client with a purchasing budget the size of a small planet and an ego to match that you ignore at your peril or the regional manager from the South West who gave up the personality correspondence course after the first week and now relies on Christmas cracker mottos as his first line in repartee.

So selecting your guest list must be a subtle mix of compromise and cunning. You want all your guests to enjoy themselves, after all that's why they're coming. But you have to expose them to the your rogues' gallery of "Must Asks". Choose wisely.

WHEN ENOUGH IS ENOUGH

Having found the excuse and drawn up the guest list, a host faces the biggest question: how far out should the boat be pushed within the bounds of budget and taste? And, what sort of boat is it in the first place?

A friend of mine recently lavished vintage champagne on his mates to such an extent that they were almost swimming in it. The only comment I heard the next day was that one or two of the guests had considered the whole thing a touch vulgar. True, you can't please all of the people all of the time, but an over-ostentatious effort puts up more backs than it scratches. Generosity can often be mistaken for arrogance.

Hosts also often make the mistake of thinking that their guests will be expecting "something different" at each and every party they go to. I agree that the Gangsters and Molls party did rather lose its appeal after the seventh outing but that doesn't mean to say that you have to come up with something totally original to please. After all, it's the people that make a party swing, not the props.

The terrifying thing for most hosts is the fact that you only get one chance to get it right. Once you've thrown open those doors there's no turning back. Fear not, some of the most spectacular parties have resulted from the most stunning cock-ups. Guests thrive on the Dunkirk spirit, pushing cars out of waterlogged car parks or manning the pumps when the bar staff fail to turn up. There is always some wag ready to do an ARP impersonation when the lights go out - and anyway, everything does look so much more romantic by candlelight. The watchword for any nervous host is "flexibility". Don't make a fuss if the caterer forgets the Batman shaped canapés, just get out there and smile - nobody will know the difference. Making a scene and getting upset will only put you and your guests on edge and that would be a disaster.

MIXING AND MINGLING

People party for the social interaction, but some are better at it than others. My father rather endearingly calls my mother his "Little Kenwood" because she is such a good mixer. "Right, I'm off to mingle," she will say on crossing the threshold and we seldom see her again 'till kicking out time. Hear her, yes. See her, no.

"Daddy, daddy. I can't find mummy."
"Well son, just stand still for a second and listen."

Like most people, I find the sight of a room full of unknown faces all jabbering away pretty daunting and I usually gravitate towards the bar where like-minded non-mixers seem to congregate. It's at this point that good hosts come into their own.

It's no good getting a group of interesting and stimulating people together unless you give them a chance to be interesting and stimulating. This often involves talking about themselves of course but then, let's be honest, that's what we all like doing best. Anyway, forcing diffident guests on each other is an art. The "Have you met so-and-so, he's from Bishops Stortford and runs a snack food factory" introduction is the host's most potent weapon. The fact that so-and-so comes from Nuneaton and runs a micro-chip company is immaterial - you've started them talking.

Hosts must never underestimate the importance of the introduction and all too often they make the mistake of assuming that sufficient quantities of alcohol will do the work for them.

Getting the party going should never be approached solely with alcohol. My father is one of the finest practitioners of the "pick-me-up" or "party warmer" but he has always found it difficult to know when to ease up on the pouring arm. His stock in trade is a mean little champagne cocktail that appears innocuous enough to the victim but it loosens the vocal chords after one sip and the inhibitions after two.

courtesy of Masquerade

I made the mistake of putting my father in charge of the drinks for what promised to be an unavoidably turgid graduation party at which my fellow graduates' parents would be present. Now, you can choose your friends but you can't pick your relatives and we had been dreading the day. As we poured the Dean's wife out of the door in the early hours singing snatches from "The Birdie Song" and attempted to revive the "just-a-small-one" retired accountant on the sofa, the old man did admit that he "may have over-done it a bit". Everybody at the time agreed that it was the best party they had been to since their own university days - but none of them has ever spoken to me again.

Lesson Two: Always let your guests know exactly what they're drinking.

THE ANSWER

So is the successful party the one where the host's agenda and the guests' expectations are met? Where everybody gets a chance to put on their party veneer and preen their party look? Well, no it isn't. Unfortunately the most successful party is the one that can't be planned. The most successful party in the world is the impromptu party where a group of you get together by pure chance when the sun is up, the wine is chilled and all is right with the world. A bit of a bummer really, considering that this is a party planning book!

Richard Hoare, Lucas Lloyd Marketing

I haven't actually had the pleasure of meeting the author's Ma or Pa but they sound well worth meeting, in contrast to many people who are thrust upon you at the corporate bash or Christmas drinks. While people are a crucial element in organising the perfect party there are so many ways of getting more from a person than you anticipate and this doesn't mean just plying them with booze.

courtesy of The Marquee Company

How do people party?

Planning a party is a very daunting experience for most people. However I love it! For the past twenty five years I have had the privilege of organising many wonderful and challenging parties, not only in the UK but worldwide: from providing Shirley Bassey as foremost entertainment in Beirut for the President, to Lionel Richie for a private party in Washington, to a large surprise custard pie fight in the UK!

What are the ingredients for making a great party? The first factor has to be the people. People make parties. You can spend the earth on your party but if you get the wrong mix of guests then you have a 'non event'. So, foremost are the guests, second comes the music. You have to have an excellent band or discothèque - they make or break a party. It really is pointless looking for the cheapest local act (unless they are excellent). You must do your research. People remember the music!

At the heart of all entertaining is good food and drink. Buffets can be great for mixing friends. Different types of food stalls - Oriental, Italian, Indian - all add to the fun of the party. Behind the scenes at parties can also be an intriguing insight into the actual production of a party - catering marquees with avenues of turbo-ovens, large walk-in fridges, full blown washing up units. Outside caterers provide first-class food as good as the top London hotels and restaurants.

Every detail is important and people remember strange things. This moves us on nicely to the subject of portaloos! It always makes me laugh. However, guests do remember the portaloos! You can now hire wonderful loos with Zoffany wallpaper, hot and cold running water and - can you believe it - real mahogany loo seats.

The party scene has changed so much over the last 25 years and I am glad to say that it has become much more professional, with the safety aspect at the front of most organisers' minds.

Theming has recently become very popular. People lose their inhibitions and this is a superb way of 'breaking the ice' at the start of parties. Recently we have transformed marquees into Caribbean islands, hotel ballrooms into an English garden complete with living statues, and an army drill hall into a Moroccan experience. The theming of parties is like a theatrical production. Many of our set designers also work in West End theatres so their attention to detail is quite superb.

Lighting always plays a very important part in any party. It creates atmosphere. Whether it is simple uplighting and pinspotting of table centres or providing stunning starcloths and projected gobos, it always creates an exciting and dramatic environment.

Last year we organised a ball for the launch of the 'Matthew' ship in Bristol. We had a sit-down dinner and dancing for 2500 guests. Apart from using four generators, each one the size of a container, we also had five hundred lamps, starcloth, three miles of cabling and a dining marquee 350ft x 80ft. These large events are challenging and exciting. In fact, the bigger the better.

I have to say that I really have had a great twenty-five years working in locations which I could not have ever dreamt of even visiting - Buckingham Palace, Windsor Castle, not forgetting stunning hotel locations and clients' own private gardens.

For me, planning my own perfect party would be simple. Forty of my best friends, excellent wines, a superb dinner and a wonderful cabaret act.

So remember, get the mix of friends right. Excellent music, nice food and drink - perhaps a theme. You then have the basis of a great party. If you are totally daunted by the whole experience, then talk to a professional.

William Bartholomew, William Bartholomew Party Organising Ltd

I recall having lunch with a rather brash Australian. He was an extremely successful businessman who also loathed flowers. We sat down and he immediately removed a beautiful floral arrangement to a nearby table. Hayfever, you ask. No, there was no good reason other than he despised anything, particularly flowers, that cluttered a table. Thankfully he is in the minority and a range of ideas to decorate tables and the other areas of a venue is seldom wasted.

Creating the right environment

Most of us use flowers, plants and perhaps trees at home to change an environment or even create a new one. Fresh flowers can brighten a dark uninviting room and an untidy corner can be transformed by a colourful plant which catches the eye to divert one's attention. Floral decorations for parties and corporate events can, through careful planning and design, have the same effect but on a much larger scale.

The single most important factor in choosing a venue is often the number of guests to be accommodated. The venue chosen sometimes leaves a certain amount to be desired in terms of ambience. Changing the environment, therefore, becomes the key to making the event a success.

Clients sometimes start off by saying "I will do the floral decorations myself", or "My wife knows all about flowers". Then there is the phone call on the day before the event to say that "Mrs Thompson has decided that 500 table centres are really too much for her after all".

The average high street florist or nursery does not have the huge range of flowers, plants and trees that the professional event supplier can call on and they are not used to the time constraints involved in these events. A late request for 100 pom-pom bay trees or 20 4m high palm trees would be impossible. Hence the importance of employing a professional who specialises in floral and theme decorations.

CHANGING THE MOOD

The challenge of large scale events is to create a more intimate atmosphere for those attending. It is important to obtain plans, dimensions, room heights and other details. Even mausoleum type function rooms with wallpaper in the worst possible taste can be transformed and softened by trees, plants and perhaps special feature areas with fountains or indoor gardens. Tropical trees, such as Ficus Benjamina or Ficus Longifolia, are ideal for venues where conditions are controlled and they are available from 1m to 5m high. Ficus trees with rounded heads or pompom shaped tops 1.5m to 2m high used along the side walls are a very effective way of lowering the height of a room if that is what is required. These

courtesy of Searcy's & Joanna Plumbe Photography

trees have straight stems, but braided stems and corkscrew spiral stems are also available and are always a talking point. To alter the mood for the evening, small white pea lights in the heads of these trees make an attractive and sophisticated addition.

Spectacular large flower arrangements are a particularly effective way to draw the eye to focal points such as the stage, reception desk or top table. Again, it is important to bear in mind the height and scale of the room.

An effective way to achieve an impression is through the use of large stone or fibreglass urns which can be either on the floor or on plinths to give the necessary height. Arrangements on decorative metal pedestals can also be effective, but be careful not to locate them where you have a lot of pedestrian traffic as they can be rather top heavy.

A good tip if you are using lilies is to ask for the stamens to be cut out. The pollen can mark clothes permanently, which may result in claims for dry cleaning.

Table centre arrangements can be designed in many different styles and it is important to give your designer as much information as possible beforehand on the nature of the event. For example, large arrangements for the tables would not be suitable for an event where guests are to remain seated while listening to after-dinner speakers - half of them wouldn't be able to see! On the other hand, low arrangements can be completely hidden when there are half a dozen wine bottles on the table. The arrangements must also be in scale with the size of the tables.

courtesy of Expo Flora Ltd

Having the right table centre for the event will help to create an intimate atmosphere at each table, even in the largest of venues. Cut flowers, dried flowers, good quality artificial flowers, fruit and even bonsai trees can all be used to create the unique effect you are looking for.

THEMED DISPLAYS

Themed displays can range from the simple use of corporate colours in the flower arrangements to, for example, a treasure island theme complete with sandy beach, coconut palms, tropical jungle and even a full scale section of a Spanish galleon. Every conceivable theme can be recreated and plants and trees add authenticity and really bring the theme alive. Specialist floral event decorators working in this area employ either full-time or part-time designers and set-dressers, usually with experience gained from the television or film industries. When it is done well, it is an unforgettable experience for guests. If done without sufficient planning and thought it is equally unforgettable but for all the wrong reasons!

It is important to bring the floral decorator into the planning process at an early stage. An effective design solution can then be found to suit your particular venue and budgetary requirements.

Above all, floral design is about creating an interesting and stimulating environment - have fun with it!

Andy Metcalf, Expo Flora Ltd

If flower power is one thing - electricity is something else and when worked in tandem the results can be truly spectacular. Whether you're hosting one thousand or a gruesome twosome, lighting can do much to make your event special and let's face it, it may be as important for the latter as it is the former!

courtesy of Searcy's & Joanna Plumbe Photography

Add impact with lighting

An event is a finished product reflecting many hours of creative thought and the accumulated talents of an entire group of professionals. Each element is crucial to the look and feel of an event, and lighting is no exception. Lighting should be designed individually for each occasion, taking into consideration the peculiarities of the venue, such as ceiling height, existing lighting, and any stage or focal points which need to be highlighted. Items such as floral arrangements within a venue need to be lit to ensure that they stand out rather than being lost in the shadows. Props, if they are being used, need to be highlighted in a way that enhances their colour and detail by using just the right amount of colour and brightness. If the event is being held at a fixed venue, architectural elements such as cornice work and columns can be enhanced by being lit as part of the overall room design.

Thought needs to be given to how lighting will be controlled for an event, as it will need to be adjusted for ambience and atmosphere to suit the mood during the course of the event. When guests arrive at a venue, the lighting needs to be at a high level to ensure a warm welcome. Usually, as guests are seated for dinner, the lighting will be adjusted to create a more intimate atmosphere. As the atmosphere develops during the evening and the after dinner music begins, the lighting will be adjusted again to draw the guests towards the dance floor. People are ill at ease and tend not to dance when they are in the glare of bright lights!

Lighting can also be very effective for the exterior of the venue. Shrubs, trees, building fascia, gazebos, pagodas, balustrades, water features, etc, can be highlighted to create a night-time wonderland. Shrubs can be lit from below, allowing the light to filter through the leaves, which in a breeze can produce a scintillating effect. A stunning effect in a garden can be created by lighting tall trees from below to increase their stature as they tower magnificently into the night sky. The use of a powerful projector positioned just far enough away to capture the top of the tree, toned with colour filters to enhance the colours of the trunk and tree canopy, will create a lasting impression on your guests.

Safety lighting is an aspect of lighting which is often overlooked. Thought needs to be given to the guests, after dining in sumptuous and well-lit surroundings, leaving the venue to find their cars. Guests have often been seen trudging through mud and water, unable to see where they are going. This generally applies to green field sites, since most fixed venues cater for this as a matter of course. Safety lighting is so important that it is mandatory at large public events where several hundred people will be leaving the site at the same time.

There are many products available today, which, when used correctly, can achieve different and exciting effects. Lighting must be specifically selected to carry out the task for which it was designed. Listed below are some of the most commonly used fittings, and any reputable lighting company will be able to tell you what effects can be achieved by each.

courtesy of Classic Lighting

- Chandeliers and wall brackets
- Uplighters
- Low voltage directional lighting
- Narrow beam pinspots
- Focusable profile fittings
- Gobos
- Starcloths
- Low voltage pealights
- Emergency lighting
- Effect/moving lighting
- Special effect lighting
- Enclosed tungsten halogen floodlights
- Fluorescent lighting
- Low bay fittings
- Colour filters
- Practical lighting
- Control equipment

SELECTING A SUPPLIER

When selecting a lighting supplier for your event, care should be taken to ensure that they:

- Are of a reputable standard
- Specialise in lighting and electrical installations
- Are, preferably, a member of a trade organisation
- Comply with the latest electrical regulations for this type of installation.

ELECTRICAL SAFETY

Outdoor events can present great problems for electrical installations, as the power supply, and possibly certain other elements of lighting installations, occasionally need to be weatherproof. Each electrical installation should be inspected and tested to ensure that it is electrically safe for the welfare of your guests and for its intended use. Prior to allowing an event to go ahead, most local authorities who licence public events will require a test certificate from a recognised association such as the National Inspection Council for Electrical Installation Contractors (NICEIC).

Where lighting is used for public events, care must be taken to protect the equipment from tampering. Self-contained tower light units used for general lighting in car park areas present tempting targets. Some people find it highly amusing to switch the units off and remove the keys, rendering them totally useless. Generators and other equipment at risk of tampering should be adequately protected using suitable barriers or enclosures.

BUYER GUIDELINES - THINGS TO LOOK FOR

- Registered with trade organisation or association
- Installations comply with the latest edition of the IEE wiring regulations
- Reputable supplier
- Obtain references for any potential suppliers
- Any proposals obtained should clearly detail fitting types and provide a description of the effects they will achieve
- Ensure that adequate space is allocated for control and dimming equipment etc
- Ensure that adequate insurance cover has been arranged

Tony Timms, Classic Lighting

courtesy of Banana Split

A good amateur is never as good as an average professional! Certain professionals know tricks of the trade that unpaid enthusiasts will not know. In catering and entertaining we all have friends who are great hosts and hostesses and some that are less auspicious. The message is that food and drink are vital but not all encompassing items in planning your special occasion, be it a weekend party or an evening of revelry. It is also clear that little things can let the side down - and they also cause the most headaches. Good preparation and attention to detail will produce better results and this advice is just as valid for the amateur as the professional.

Ingredients for the perfect party

What does make the perfect party?

Is it the people, music, venue, theming or a combination of all these elements?

The best parties are those where the hosts enjoy themselves as much as their guests and memories of the party are still bubbling long after the champagne has gone flat.

To create a perfect occasion you need the perfect ingredients. Everyone wants their event to run smoothly and with as little stress, aggravation and hassle as possible. Apart from an essential party checklist, the key to a great event is in creating the right atmosphere, and it is at this point that you should decide whether a professional outfit should be employed. There are many different types of party planners available, but the key to making your event successful is finding one who works in partnership with you. The party planner must listen to your requirements and devise an event that is tailor-made to your own requirements and budget.

The beauty of dealing with an experienced outfit is their ability to make you feel relaxed yet still in control. You can choose to let them run the whole event or you can cherry-pick the services you require - the band or cabaret, the marquee, theming and balloons, etc.

The initial stages of party planning must establish the purpose of the event. Is it a birthday, anniversary, wedding or a themed corporate function? This will help decide other elements of the essential 'party checklist'. Is the venue to be a marquee, a hotel or another outside location? Do you want theming, catering, music, decor, cabaret, flowers, balloons? What about car parking, invitations, RSVPs, photography, videos, leaving gifts?

Clearly not every element of a party can be controlled, nor would anyone want to control every element. Careful planning can take care of the controllable elements, leaving the hosts to enjoy their own event. Story boards are often drawn to illustrate the combined effect of all the elements, and a time plan of the event is produced to ensure that the function runs as smoothly as possible and to accurate time scales.

Most parties are over too quickly and all that is left are memories and anecdotes, so a photographer can be a beneficial addition to your event. A picture is worth a thousand words!

Party and special event organisers can design the total 'party package'. This can include everything from tailor-made marquees, sound systems and discothèques to gourmet food. Floral decorations, photography, video, celebrity acts and cabaret can be arranged. Events can be themed with specially designed balloons, spectacular laser shows and fireworks. They offer a complete professional service for any event, however large or small, and they are creative and organised.

The key to organising a party is to enjoy the planning period as well as the event itself. If you decide to employ a party or event organiser, make sure you will enjoy working with them and that your event will be important to them. If the hosts are happy and relaxed, if they have time to circulate, chat and have fun, then the party organiser has done a good job. They should enable the client to feel confident and relaxed as the organisation and stress is taken out of their hands.

By the time the lights come on and the champagne starts flowing, the client can sit back, join their guests and enjoy the fun.

Banana Split

Probably the best party I've attended was, on the face of it, extremely chic… a black and white affair, but it was special and beautifully organised from the starcloths in the marquee to the garden, which had been delicately transformed into a black and white mini paradise. The food, music and entertaining all revolved around the venue… attention to detail was prodigious and the memory lives on like a burning white beacon, a never fading memory !

While attention to detail in any part of life always produces favourable results, this is especially true when bringing people together, be it for business or pleasure or both. In order to be a success there are some items you simply cannot ignore.

Planning the party

A party can be an occasion to celebrate a wide range of events, anything from clinching a business deal to a christening, so one of the first things to consider is what you wish to achieve by arranging the party in the first place.

If the party is for a relatively small number you may consider doing the catering for it yourself. In this case, simplicity generally works best because at the end of the day you want to enjoy the occasion as much as your guests. It is all very well producing a buffet table groaning with delicious delicacies but who is going to go around the room picking up plates and finding all the bits of food wedged down the side of the sofa, and then do an hour or so of washing up? Not the best recipe for a fun party for you.

If you do not feel confident about catering for your own party, I would strongly advise that you employ a caterer to do it for you. Word of mouth is the best way to find your caterer. Discuss with them over the telephone what you want and ask their advice on what will work best with the facilities and budget you have. Get a minimum of two quotations and meet with the caterers before you decide. The cost-per-head is not the only consideration. Try to find out exactly what is included and also the standard to which they operate. This is where personal recommendation is so crucial. Find a friend with tastes and expectations similar to your own and go from there.

It is fatal to get carried away with a wonderful sounding, exotic menu which you may love, only to find that your friends and relations spend the whole time trying to recognise what they are eating and cannot wait to nip out to the pub for a simple meal. Plan the menu around the range of people you are going to entertain. There is nothing wrong with exotic menus but always think about your guests.

The points to consider when organising a party do tend to apply to both large and small events.

- What are you celebrating? Is it formal, business, casual, family, etc?

- Employ a caterer that is highly recommended but, more importantly, one you feel comfortable with, as they are going to play a large part in your celebrations. This is not the time for a clash of personalities.

- If catering for the event yourself, plan the menu realistically. Consider your budget, your capabilities and work space and, most importantly, adequate refrigeration. Do not remove your chicken mayonnaise dish to make room to chill those lovely bottles of champagne - fatal move.

- Help - even if you decide to produce the food yourself, find someone to come and wash up for you for a few hours. It will make your party for you.

- Logistics - How many people can you accommodate? Consider carefully both the space and the budget available. Perhaps you should think about hiring a small marquee with tables and chairs.

- Always plan on the weather being wet. This IS Great Britain!. Do not think you can automatically have fifty people to lunch sitting at tables in the garden. What happens when the heavens open? Disaster.

- Cater for children with small, fun food. It is advisable to feed them first, then they will be happy to play while the parents enjoy their lunch. A bouncy castle hidden somewhere in the grounds or an entertainer will keep them happy for hours!

- If the party is in the evening and with music, always notify your neighbours and tell them what time the music will stop. Better still, invite them. For large parties, it is advisable to mention it to your local policeman especially if you live in a small village as the whole village may complain about the noise!

- Parking - Try to accommodate cars safely off the roads and do not block neighbours' driveways.

- Entertainment - If you are hiring a live band or a disco, it is advisable to hear them play and discuss what music they play, etc. You also want to know how many breaks they have and if they play CDs when resting.

- Decoration - There are various ways to decorate a room or marquee. For a fun party, balloons can be very effective. Get some ideas from balloon companies and from florists, ask to see photographs of their work.

- Loos - Not a problem for a small party, but it is worth spending some money on a decent mobile trailer loo for larger parties. The marquee company can attach the marquee to the mobile loos so your guests are not left stumbling across a damp field at 2 am to find the loo.

- A point to consider, especially with a wedding when people get to know what time the whole family will be away from the house, is to ensure that you leave someone responsible in the house to deter any unwanted visitors!

- It is worth writing down answers to the above points when planning your party. It may seem like a lot of unnecessary work at the time, but planning in the early stages will make the party a success and enable you to relax and enjoy it.

Kaye Thompson, The Creative Catering Company

courtesy of Dennis Ramsey

Pleasing floral effects

Since early times, flowers have been symbolic but it was the Victorians who turned the giving and using of flowers into an art-form. Each flower had its own meaning and presentation also became very important.

These days we no longer pick our flowers from field and hedgerow and few today know the language of flowers which our grandparents and their parents all knew so well. Only a few examples are well known: red roses for love, Lily of the Valley for happiness, white lilies for purity, and of course Forget-Me-Not as its name suggests.

Flowers can add so much to your special event, whether it be small nosegays with ribbons and lace for a christening, superb arrangements of white lilies, roses and gladioli for a wedding, or a riot of colours and species for a special birthday party. Decoration can vary from the simple and inexpensive to the lavish and profuse. Whichever is chosen, with the use of swags, ribbons, pots of blooms in assorted containers, and, of course, armfuls of flowers, the scene is set!

Here are some simple but pleasing effects you might consider:

- Co-ordinate the table arrangements with the tablecloths and napkins
- Incorporate seasonal fruit and berries with the flowers
- Hanging balls of flowers
- Swag trees
- Freeze flower heads into ice cubes. They look attractive in a glass bowl waiting to be used and also as floating decorations.

Russell Twining & Bere Ltd

courtesy of Searcy's & Joanna Plumbe Photography

The language of flowers

Acacia, Friendship
Almond blossom, Encouragement
Aloe, Grief
Anemone, Soul of goodness
Apple blossom, You are preferred
Arbutus, I love but thee
Balm, Sympathy
Bee Orchid, Industry
Begonia, Steadfast
Blackthorn, Courage under trials
Bluebell, True and tender
Borage, There are obstacles
Bramble, Perserverance
Buttercup, Homeliness
Calceolaria, Don't be jealous
Camellia, Beautiful but cold
Carnation—White, Purity
Carnation—Deep Red, My heart is broken
Celandine, Be not down-hearted
Chrysanthemum, Hope springs eternal
Clematis, Poor but honest
Clover—Red, Sweetness
Columbine, Bound to win
Convolvulus, Hearts entwined
Cornflower, Never despair
Cowslip, Happiness
Crocus, Ever glad
Cypress, Affliction
Daffodil, Welcome
Dahlia, Gracious
Daisy, Innocence
Daphne, Immortality
Eglantine, I am cruel to be kind
Fennel, Strength
Fern, Sincerity
Forget-me-not, Forget-me-not
Foxglove, Deceitful
Fuchsia, Fickleness
Gentian, Hope
Geranium, Warm regard
Gorse, Constancy
Grass of Parnassus, I dream of thee
Harebell, Short-lived joy
Hawthorn, Courage in adversity
Heather, I am lonely
Holly, Rejoice together
Honeysuckle, Devotion
Hyacinth, Hard fate Iris, Have faith in me
Ivy, I cling
Jasmine, Friends only
Laburnum, Forsaken

Laurel, Triumph
Lavender, Sweets to the sweet
Lilac, Unadorned beauty
Lily, Austere purity
Lily of the Valley, Doubly dear
Lime, Domestic bliss
Lobelia, Unselfishness
London Pride, Unassuming
Magnolia, Magnamity
Maple, Do not forget
Marigold, Honesty
Mignonette, Undiluted pleasure
Mint, Riches
Musk Rose, You charm me
Myrrh, Happiness
Myrtle, Unforgotten joys
Nasturtium, Optimism
Olive, Peace
Orange blossom, Happiness in marriage
Palm, Victory
Pansy, Thoughts
Passion Flower, Comfort in affliction
Petunia, I believe in thee
Pimpernel, Consolation
Polyanthus, Unreasoning pride
Poppy, Forgetfulness
Primrose, Do not be bashful
Primrose—Evening , Duplicity
Rose—Red, Love
Rose—White, Worthy of love
Rose—Yellow, Why waneth love?
Rosemary, Remembrance
Sage, Virtuous and wise
St. John's Wort, Real nobility
Sensitive Plant, Fain would I climb
Sheperd's Purse, Pride of worth
Snowdrop, Goodness unalloyed
Speedwell, God be with you
Starwort, Second thoughts are better
Strawberry blossom, Patience and
foresight
Sunflower, Adoration
Sweet Pea, I long for thee
Sweet William, Pleasant dreams
Thistle, Defence not defiance
Thyme, Affection
Tulip, Unrequited love
Verbena, You have my confidence
Violet, Modesty
Wallflower, Loyalty in friendship
White Heather, Good luck

To conclude this introductory chapter, I recall what to me was the finest party I was involved with. It was a spectacle organised in London at the Honourable Artillery Club - it was called The Big Bang City Ball. 1250 people attended. Everything was quite outstanding, with four marquees being used, each with a seasonal theme. Some major companies were heartily promoting their products and the evening lacked nothing . . . well almost nothing. The problem was the organiser had expected to sell 2000 tickets and some of the bars (there were 16) and some of the dance floors (there were 4) were underused - the atmosphere was shining but it didn't buzz. It only goes to show that no matter how brilliant the planning, the catering and the entertainment, it is the people who provide the greatest colour and enjoyment!

EVENT MANAGEMENT FOR MARKETING & MOTIVATION

ELEGANT DAYS LIMITED

Since 1983 Elegant Days has been a leading supplier of high quality sports hospitality packages and bespoke corporate events.

◆ Full sporting calendar

◆ All-inclusive packages

◆ One-stop hospitality solutions

◆ Tailor-made dinners & receptions

◆ All CHA & HSE guidelines applied

Elegant Days has been voted the Corporate Hospitality & Event Association's Event Management Company of the Year for two successive years for 1996 and 1997

ELEGANT DAYS BROCHURE UPDATE
CALL 01926 842044 or 0171 736 7772

Business

For Business and Pleasure

Alexander Pope, a canny fellow by all accounts, said in a letter to E. Blount in 1714: "Party spirit, which at best is but the madness of many for the gain of a few". Now the old master may well have a point. If you've ever been entertained at a sporting event or corporate thrash then it is difficult not to conclude that your short-term happiness must be put aside for the subsequent gain of others. Such an attitude, however, is somewhat jaundiced - some people actually like to say thank you and in business it's as important to look after the friends you have as to fret about those you are yet to meet.

Planning a corporate event

An outstanding corporate event can really raise the profile of your company's business success. Here are Sam Chalmers' tips for planning a first class occasion for valued clients.

Early planning is crucial for a carefree occasion. Make a schedule of everything that needs to be done before the big day and another detailed, minute by minute timetable for the day itself.

Ensure that the event you have chosen is in accordance with the season; for example, horse racing in April can be cold and blustery. To maximise the number of acceptances, avoid selecting a date in the most popular periods for vacations - typically around the school holidays.

If you are approaching a celebrity to attend, make this one of your first tasks and think of more than one possibility in case your first choice is already booked.

Think about whether a lunchtime or evening event is most desirable and which day of the week would appeal most to your guests. Daytime entertainment is often preferred by corporate guests attending without partners - and it's more economical for the host. An evening function could mean the extra expense of hotel rooms.

Mondays or Tuesdays are often thought too pressured at work for people to accept invitations and on Fridays their thoughts are on the weekend. Consider the needs of your guests - if it's a family occasion such as a garden party make sure there is entertainment for the children.

Put a highly efficient member of staff in charge of the invitation list and RSVPs. When designing the invitation, ask guests to respond by a certain date and to say if they have any special dietary requirements.

When considering which party planner to hire, ask to see a list of clients they have worked for in the recent past and any letters of praise. Look at the different menus offered and remember that simple flavoursome dishes are always best. Check that all raw ingredients used are of the highest quality. A cold starter can be placed on the tables before people are seated which means less fuss, and if you are catering for large numbers, don't pick soup.

Talk to your party organiser about the theme of your event - it could easily be incorporated into the decoration of the venue and even the food itself. Follow your theme through invitations to the table settings but keep in mind that 'less is more' - don't go over the top! Discuss with your event manager whether seating at one table or in small groups is most appropriate. You may wish to reserve a table for VIP guests.

The catering company should know to keep the glasses filled and it's thoughtful to provide interesting non-alcoholic drinks for those who are driving, or who don't drink.

Space for parking cars, enough lavatories, clear signage and facilities to leave coats must also be considered. Think about where the catering company will site their kitchen - a special tent is usual if you are hiring a marquee.

When the replies come in, send guests a map of how to reach the event, a brochure if the party is at a historic house or racecourse, and a list of any dress rules.

As the day draws nearer, check, check and check again that all aspects of the event are proceeding to plan and have been covered. And on the day itself, don't forget about yourself. Take time to dress carefully, appearing confident and relaxed. There's nothing worse than a stressed-out host.

Sam Chalmers, Chimneys Outside Catering Company and Chimneys Restaurant

Sport absorbs some and angers others - its addictive nature captures millions and others wonder what it is all about. As one who is addicted to it, the opportunity to be entertained at Twickenham, Lords or Ascot is most appealing. In a nutshell there are sporting events that are great spectacles and there are many others of a less captivating nature. To many aficionados, business entertaining at the great events is a disgrace. Why give a valuable seat to the Chairman's wife who hates cricket? . . . fair point. But the reason why this corporate entertaining lark will not be given up is because it works, it really works. An opportunity is given to attend something special, to provide good food and drink and if needs be to dot the 'i's and cross the 't's of a deal . . . but usually it's just generating acquaintances.

Partying at sporting events

The human animal is both social and competitive, and so the concepts of sport and partying are entirely complementary. Indeed there is a sport of social climbing, of which partying is an essential element, and this only serves to prove the point. Whenever there is sport, there is cause for celebration or commiseration and the natural vehicle to express either is the party.

The recent World Cup was described as the Greatest Party on Earth. In 1999 we have two more World Cups so one can only assume that this represents the most stupendous Party on Earth times two. This image does carry risks: the media perception of the Greatest Party on Earth may be bars heaving with drunks, hooligans hurling bottles, and a rubbish mountain the size of Everest. For most of us, however, partying at sporting events represents a gathering of like-minded souls enjoying company, hospitality and an opportunity to take part vicariously in great competition whilst avoiding the training, the physical exertion and, in many cases, the expense.

Planning a party at a sports event is relatively simple. Most sports venues offer hospitality facilities or packages, and if these are inappropriate or beyond your pocket, the picnic around the boot of the car is broadly the same at Royal Ascot, Twickenham or Burghley Horse Trials.

The important elements of the party are who you invite, what you eat, where you meet, what you see, and where you see it from. Knowledge of the sport is not paramount but would be helpful, and the guest list should include an "expert". He will enjoy the event as the adulation will inflate his ego; the other guests may enjoy it but they will certainly enjoy competing with him. From the hosts' point of view, the "expert" will relieve them of the responsibility of dispensing knowledge, leaving them free to concentrate on the important issue of the day: the menu.

courtesy of Cameo Photography

As with all parties, it is important to identify any special dietary requirements well in advance. It is impossible to find kosher at Kempton, gluten-free at Gloucester or vegan anywhere at short notice. Similarly there will always be someone who drinks only brandy or Diet Coke, and foreknowledge is invaluable. Most sporting venues are not well equipped for last minute requests. Otherwise the menu should take into account the style of the event, the time of year and possibly the sport. The menu will inevitably reflect on the host, and it is best if it reflects well.

Once your guests have accepted the invitation, they need foolproof joining instructions. Most guests attending an event go into some form of autopilot under which they assume either that you will beam them directly from home to your party, or that every car park attendant knows you personally and will lead them to your party by hand if necessary.

Joining instructions should identify the date, the time, the venue, which car park or drop off point to use, and give some indication of what to expect once the guests get there. You can have a great party on Pimms and cucumber sandwiches, but if your guests were expecting a three-course lunch they might not think so. Joining instructions should also include a dress code, emergency contact number and a timetable of events.

When guests arrive, the traditional party skills will be required: introducing people, explaining what is going to happen and when, and ensuring there is a steady flow of food and drink prior to the sport. It is bad form to miss the sport altogether, but worse to eat and drink and spectate at the same time. There are exceptions, of course (greyhound racing being one), but generally it is wise to party before, spectate during and celebrate afterwards.

courtesy of Banana Split

Etiquette is important at sporting events. Indeed it is so important that if ignored it can cause embarrassment and even put a dampener on the whole event. Embarrassment at social functions is feared by all and the host should go to great lengths to reduce any chance of it occurring. Explain the dress code relevant to your party, explain the bounds of the admission ticket and identify any eccentricities of the particular sport. For example, treading the divots at polo or walking the course at cross country is to be encouraged, but a similar approach to Glorious Goodwood or the Formula One at Silverstone would be dangerous and embarrassing. Wearing tails at Royal Ascot is essential in the Royal Enclosure, encouraged in the Boxes, but embarrassing in the Silver Ring. It is wise to delicately point guests in the right direction and avoid any potential embarrassment on the day.

The success of the party will be assured if the sportsmen excel. But if the host has followed all the guidelines, even a wet weekend in Wigan can become a Perfect Party.

Eddie Hoare, Elegant Days

courtesy of Searcy's & Joanna Plumbe Photography

Entertaining at sporting events

Imagine this. It's the big day at the RAC British Grand Prix at Silverstone. It is very early in the morning and hundreds of people are squeezing into the circuit for a day of excitement. People are rushing to find the best spot from which to view the action.

You, on the other hand, are casually ambling over to one of the Sellers ArenaScene structures which overlook either the Vale Straight or the Pits at Copse. On arrival after your fraught journey to the circuit, you are greeted warmly and shown to the luxuriously furnished box which is to be your home for the day. Here you are supplied with breakfast. You make yourself comfortable either reading one of the newspapers supplied for you or meandering onto the balcony to watch the circuit parades and warm-ups, and before you know it the champagne has arrived.

After an extremely satisfying four-course luncheon, served with very fine wines and topped off with a glass or two of port or brandy, you can feel the tension begin to mount. You walk a few paces out onto your balcony where the spectacle is unbeatable as Damon Hill and Michael Schumacher come speeding towards you.

courtesy of Burghley House

It is hard to believe that you are in a temporary hospitality suite. These purpose-built structures are fully equipped with balconies, kitchens, televisions, heaters or air-conditioners and toilets. They are moved from venue to venue throughout the year, and every year thousands of guests enjoy the best of the action coupled with superb hospitality in the comfort of these Sellers ArenaScene glass-fronted suites.

Hospitality with Sellers ArenaScene is not restricted to those bringing large numbers of guests. Each venue can cater for one or two people within the restaurant facilities. Large groups of guests or corporate clients can be accommodated in individual private suites for twenty-four, thirty-two or forty-eight guests depending upon availability.

Charles Webb, Sellers ArenaScene Ltd

Whether you are having a small party at home, putting up a marquee in the garden or using another location altogether, there are several basic rules you should follow–and planning and communication are two of the most significant. In considering whether to stay at home or go further afield there are numerous items to consider.

Choosing a party venue

There are thousands of "Other Locations". Many can be found in the back of this book. My own company, Searcy's, lists some 100 or so venues in our booklet "Prestigious Venues" (free on enquiry), with various classifications and gradings.

When asked - as we are at least a dozen times a day - where to hold an event, we always try to elicit from our prospective customer various facts:

- What is the occasion?
- What is the objective or purpose of the event?
- What approximate numbers are expected to attend?
- What is the format of the occasion? (i.e. a seated served dinner, a buffet supper, a seminar, a conference, a reception and so on)

Each of the answers to these questions will prompt more questions. These will relate mainly to the format. This is not just because we, as a catering firm, need to know the type of menu suggestions to send but because, based on these answers, we are then able to recommend a carefully selected list of potentially suitable venues.

I had considered setting out a table of questions and answers for all types of venues for the purposes of this article, but realised that it would - if properly compiled - be bigger than this book! A few thoughts then.

The format and numbers will usually be the biggest determining factor. Here are some others:

- **Geographical Area** - Where do you want to hold the party? There may be limiting factors for some events. For example, you need to be within easy travelling distance of the church in the case of a wedding party.

- **Times** - There are many locations that don't allow parties after a given time, say 11 pm.

- **Dancing** - Some venues don't allow this at all for a variety of reasons. Is dancing crucial or just a 'nice to have'?

- **Smoking** - Many places don't allow this for understandable reasons. Is it important to you as a considerate host that your guests be allowed to smoke?

- **Availability** - Various places are booked up 2 or 3 years in advance, very often because they only allow a very limited number of events per year. Apsley House or Spencer House (both in Central London) fall into this category. Other places, such as City of London Livery Halls, all close in August. Many venues are not available on Saturdays.

- **Capacity** - When you are asking a venue how many guests it can handle, be sure that you have worked out how many will actually accept as opposed to being invited. (As a rough rule of thumb allow for 30% refusals. Certain other constraints apply too. If both families involved in a wedding live locally to the venue, the acceptance ratio is likely to be higher.) Also, consider how many people you want to be seated (all of them, half of them, a third of them and so on).

- **Attitude** - Do the people you're dealing with seem to want you to hold your party there? Although this seems simplistic, during the lead up to your event it will probably be the single biggest difference between whether the detailed planning of your event is fun or a burden. Is it - sorry for the phrase - a "user-friendly" place?

- **Experience** - Has this venue handled this type of occasion before? Have you really conveyed to them what your requirements are? Did they seem to understand them and be sympathetic to them?

- **Contractors** - Will the Venue Manager be helpful over the arrangements for other contractors such as florists or lighting firms? Does the venue need a lot of lighting? In my own experience £100 of lighting does more to brighten up a drab venue than £100 of flowers any time.

- **Security** - Is it too tight or too slack? Is the main priority of the venue some other purpose? An obvious example is an historic house whose year-round trade from visitors is more important to them than your one event, and they would be silly to jeopardise that in order to comply with your specific requests.

- **Other Restrictions** - There could be lots. There could be restrictions on the list of permitted contractors. There could be - well, lots and lots more. Be sure you know them before going too far with your planning.

I really could write a book on each of these aspects, as there are so many pitfalls that I've seen people fall into or narrowly avoid over the years.

courtesy of Dennis Ramsey

If I had to give one single piece of advice it would be, I think, to listen to the venue manager, once you have selected your venue. He - or she - will have seen and experienced parties of a similar type to yours before. He will have seen the way in which people flow around that particular venue. They can't all be right all of the time, obviously. As a contractor and as a venue manager I've seen - and committed - some real howlers in my time. By and large though the venue manager will have much more experience than you about precisely the subjects you want to cover that it is at least worth listening to him/her.

One more caveat though on the same subject. Watch out for the venue manager who agrees to everything too easily or too reluctantly. And above all watch out for the one who wants to create his/her own party without listening to you or trying to understand what you want. Parties are about people. You will know what type of people your guests are. Use the venue manager to help you create the right atmosphere for them.

Freddie Meynell, Searcy's

courtesy of Searcy's & Joanna Plumbe Photography

Although an Englishman's home may be his castle, it is sometimes a benefit, particularly when arranging a party, to borrow someone else's. This allows a whole range of other options that are simply not possible when planning a party at your own home. There are obvious occasions such as sporting or cultural happenings (Glyndebourne or the Grand-Prix spring to mind) but there are hundreds of other options from the local scout hall to the London Science Museum. There is today, more than ever, an array of locations that are keen to attract the private or the corporate party - the only difficulty arises in choosing the right one for your requirements. What follows are a few words of wisdom to think about when considering whether to have a party away from the family castle.

Why choose a stately home

There can be little doubt that it is very difficult to recreate that intimate house party when entertaining business colleagues or friends and family away from home. However, it is clear that this is ultimately what we all wish to achieve and is essential in making a party so memorable.

Among others, Weston Park offers an environment to meet this desire. It is a beautiful home with all the original family heirlooms, collections and paintings by grand masters. Although a magnificent stately home in every sense, the house is not too grand or stately in feel. A warm, welcoming ambience greets you as you walk in the front door and any host or hostess wishing to conjure up a fantasy of welcoming their guests to their home will not be disappointed.

But why would you consider a house like this when you could go to a club or stately hotel with all those modern trappings - branded health spa, room service, fine dining restaurant etc? Because you can never truly feel that the property is yours and you will always be one of many guests, rather than having that subtle feeling that you are one of the very few that have had the opportunity to stay.

Service is always very individual - your party will always be the only party. So many treasures are here to be enjoyed in a very personal way. Gardens and parkland meticulously maintained and preserved as when they were designed so long ago. Menu, wines, allocation of bedrooms all personally chosen by you, the host, and our house staff are available throughout your stay.

courtesy of Weston Park

"As soon as I set eyes on Weston I knew I had found the perfect property. I decided to exploit the character of the place by giving the whole event a 'house party' theme and the people at Weston Park could not have done more to co-operate".

Ironically, although the house may not have all the convenience of a modern hotel there is still an inherent flexibility to the venue - laying on everything from hot air ballooning to horse riding. You may even discuss with our head gardener the individual house plants you would like to have waiting in your guests' bedrooms!

HINTS & TIPS

- The little touches make all the difference - flowers (colour, size - not too intrusive to conversation or eye contact)

- Dietary options may be personally selected

- Do not structure your stay too rigidly. Allow people the chance to enjoy their surroundings. Do not provide so much entertainment or activity that it takes over.

Whilst a balloon festival is probably the most weather dependent activity, there is no doubt that the visual impact of 25-30 giant balloons - of varying unusual shapes and designs - is a breathtaking sight on a balmy summer's evening.

It is this romantic vision that can make a balloon festival so appealing as the basis of a dedicated festival and is an ideal as the family day out. However finding the ideal location, in terms of access, aesthetic value, and support facilities, is key to the event's success. Given that our climate can wreak havoc with flights it is also important that thoughtful planning is implemented to ensure that there are plenty of activities and entertainment for the family to enjoy. The great British public still enjoys the

opportunity to browse around traditional arts and crafts, be amazed by professional animal displays, marching bands, parachute displays, funfairs and the ever present clown. Communication is the key and a good compère will keep everyone happy, informed, and will smooth over any last minute, unforeseen changes to the programme.

The festival planner must apply a sense of fun with a keen eye for organisation and detail. Outside contractors for every different aspect need to be co-ordinated and the success of an event will hinge on the time dedicated to this at the very beginning of the planning stage.

Never forget that, as well as your visitor having an enjoyable experience, all the people who contribute to the show must also be listened to, assisted and looked after. A well-selected location will have an influence on all of these. Similarly, a professional support team both at an administrative and operational level should help you highlight the pitfalls and support you in implementing your plans.

It is this team of people that will help co-ordinate publicity, legal obligations, liaison with local authorities, contact with police, traffic control etc.

As with any event, whether it be a private party with friends or a public occasion for several thousand it is very often the little touches that make all the difference:

- Signage
- Parking
- Toilets
- Courtesy vehicles
- Specialist catering
- Clearly laid out site
- Planned, dedicated locations for contractors
- Wet weather provisions
- Dedicated show organiser to oversee and co-ordinate the entire event

Weston Park

The scientific solution

Imagine planning a stress free party - no desperate search for the right caterer, no worrying whether the flowers will arrive on time, the lighting is perfect, the entertainment is original, the location is stunning, the ambience is just right - and it's all organised for you!

This may sound too good to be true, but if your aim is to achieve the perfect party that is original, stress free and a real success then choosing a venue other than your home or office environment is the only solution.

The Science Museum in London has been helping to plan and hold events for many years, with a highly accomplished team of events professionals at hand to help you plan your event at every stage. Years of proven experience mean that our in-house team is ideally placed to recommend outside specialists for every aspect of event planning: from catering to lighting; from sound systems to entertainers. Their collective expertise ensures that when it comes to organising memorable events absolutely nothing is left to chance.

Space is an important consideration when you are planning your event. For most people any more than 15 guests for dinner or 30 for a reception would mean a logistical nightmare in one's own home. Finding an alternative venue is therefore imperative and choosing the right venue is the key to success. When selecting a venue one also has to consider atmosphere, location and aesthetics, and getting the right combination is a difficult task.

Thinking laterally and holding your event somewhere a little more unusual than a hotel or conference centre is often the perfect solution to this dilemma. Locations such as a museum, a castle or an art gallery can offer inspiring interiors which one would never encounter in a purpose-built venue. Interesting surroundings create such a talking point that even the most shy guests can find something to talk about.

An extraordinary event is likely to be remembered for much longer than a run-of-the-mill party. If you are holding a corporate event this can be so important - your clients may be invited to several events over, for example, the Christmas period. After a couple of drinks all corporate dos start to blur into one - the same people, the same food, the same tedious surroundings. Imagine how much more likely your guests would be to remember your party, and therefore your business, if it was there that they had tried out a flight simulator, wandered through a tropical rainforest or watched an enactment of a mediaeval battle. It's not just corporate affairs that benefit from this kind of originality. There's nothing better than having a birthday party or anniversary that your friends talk about for years to come.

courtesy of The Ice Box

Making your party special is easy when you have both a great location and an experienced events team at hand to make your ideas become reality. When experienced professionals take charge of an event it leaves you free to do the socialising or networking that you would really like to be doing. It would be a shame to listen to all your friends talking about what a great party you threw when your only memory is of running around fretting about every detail. Why not enjoy the party without having to worry, and then let someone else tidy up afterwards!

Joanna Rynhold, Science Museum

What type of service?

SERVED MEAL

Advantages:
- Everything is under your catering manager's control
- Everybody is paced at the same speed so that the meal can be timed
- The food and service are more like a restaurant
- This is the most formal service, and exactly right for many events
- Everybody has a seat
- You can effect a 'placement' - in other words you can allocate guests to tables

Disadvantages:
- It is a bit 'flat'. Unless you move either the men or the women after the main course, they only talk to the same few guests all evening
- This service needs the most staff - a minimum of one food waiter per table of 10 and one wine waiter (who can help with sauces etc) for 30

FORK BUFFET

Advantages:
- Good social interaction
- You can provide a menu that everybody can eat
- This form of service is usually the cheapest

Disadvantages:
- Unless you use 'plate clips' it is difficult to balance everything. (Mind you, I know two members of the Royal Family who go around with one of our plate clips permanently in their pocket or handbag so they don't get caught out!)
- Guests get tired more quickly and so the party finishes earlier
- If there are any elderly guests, the lack of seating can be torture for them. However, despite this, don't provide chairs for more than about one-third of the guests or it will look as if you have simply miscalculated

SEATED BUFFET

Advantages:
- This is cheaper than a served meal providing you don't offer too much choice
- Everybody has a seat
- You can effect a 'placement', in other words you can allocate guests to tables
- You can provide a menu that everybody can eat
  (A GOLDEN RULE: Always have a laid up starter for this type of meal. If you don't, on the announcement of the meal guests will be queuing up at the buffet table(s) for hours before they get anything to eat. Have a pretty starter already at each guest's place. I promise you it all ends in an untidy mess if you ignore this.)
- Guests need only go to the buffet table(s) once. The dessert (if restricted to one or two items) and coffee can be served to the tables.

Disadvantages:
- If you are not careful, the cost of the food alone can be much more than a served meal, and the whole event can end up costing more even though there are fewer staff.

Freddie Meynell, Searcy's

Special venues

What do we look for when we are asked to light a venue? Most initial sightings take place either in daylight, or, if there are few or no windows, when the venue is lit functionally (usually fundamental public access). Many of today's venues are not lit for 'party' mood simply because they are not primarily party venues. They are museums, public buildings, palaces, civic halls, shops - all places where the day-to-day emphasis is on agendas other than entertaining.

Often then, the initial approach to lighting these venues is to switch off all the existing lights and begin again.

What is already in place? Have a look at the space you are using and decide what lighting would make the room itself interesting. Are there pillars or architectural features that could be uplit? Does it have unusual features, perhaps statues, that might be spotlit? Is there an interesting roof or beams or paintings that could be enhanced with a soft wash? Do any of these features look as though colour would improve or add a little drama to their appearance? Perhaps, by virtue of being featureless, the walls would benefit from having streaks of light shining up them, thus creating features?

courtesy of Fisher

What we are trying to construct is an ambient, low level of light using definite and separate component parts.

Whereas in marquees you start from scratch and build to your own agenda, in venues the first objective is to fit a lighting design into established parameters. You will probably not have the flexibility of installation positions to hang the lamps exactly where you'd like. You may find yourself trimming your proposed scheme to fit within the limits of the available power supply, rather than bringing in a generator. Cabling cannot be hidden behind the lining in a brick and plaster room, so even the physical aspects of the installation require more discipline and detail.

These and other restrictions of the 'don't touch the paintwork', 'no tape to be used' and 'all fittings to be free-standing' variety all add to the challenge of working in special venues. In spite of this the mission remains the same: to present the space in a way that it has not been seen before. It is rewarding to hear the comment 'I wish this room always looked like this' from those people, security guards, managers, etc, who see the room day in and day out and notice the difference.

Fisher

courtesy of Dennis Ramsey

One of the delights of entertaining is that you don't have to be over-ambitious or vastly wealthy to have fun. The combination of good catering, a funfair and people willing to party has made for some storming evenings and at a remarkably low cost… often when planning parties the simplest cocktail is the best received.

All the fun of the fair

Many of the best corporate events now include a variety of quality funfair equipment and attractions for clients. These provide pro-active entertainment for guests who may not want to dance or take advantage of the karaoke opportunities but who still want to do more than stand drinking and talking all evening. There is a bit of a child in everyone, and everyone enjoys the fun of the fair.

You might be surprised at how easy it is to fit elements of a funfair into either indoor or outdoor spaces. People tend to think of funfair attractions as being large - the Dodgems, the Big Wheel, or the Carousels. But even if the space available is small, it is still possible to experience the thrill and excitement, and the colours, lights and sounds of the funfair. Virtual reality and video games, traditional funfair sideshows and mini-rides can all be tucked into the smallest halls and rooms. Such unlikely places as corridors, halls and lobbies have all been equipped to recreate the feel of Victorian fairgrounds complete with period "Test of Strength" hammer and bells.

Giving a client the best possible creative ideas is more than a simple question of measuring space, ordering attractions, siting and operating them. It is all about listening to the client's ideas and aspirations, and then working with them and within their budget to turn their ideas into reality. In this way even a tight space can be used to enhance a function and provide active entertainment for guests in a way that will surprise and delight them.

courtesy of Dennis Ramsey

SCENE AND HEARD

Set designers working on corporate events often look for traditional and easy answers to their client's needs without considering more imaginative alternatives, even where these would add to the quality of the event and save money. An area frequently overlooked is the possibility of using parts of the actual funfair equipment to provide lighting and music.

Top quality rides include complex and sophisticated lighting systems and high quality sound systems. By properly laying out and adapting the rides themselves to fit into the chosen theme, the budget for decking can be reduced and channelled into improving what is after all a fundamental part of the event. The budget is being used for pro-active parts of the event and not merely for decorative items.

This approach can work particularly well indoors. Funfair rides can be used to visually lower the height of high-ceilinged halls. The integral lighting of the funfair rides can be used instead of spotlights to focus attention on the rides and away from 'dead spaces'. In large enough spaces, the attractions can be laid out to form a corridor through which guests pass. Unlike scenery, these are live and active pathways offering opportunities for fun as well as visual pleasure.

35

Hiring a funfair attraction can add enormously to your event without adding enormously to your budget. For instance a set of Deluxe Dodgems provides a stage, lighting, sound system, PA, music and entertaiment all for around the price you would pay just to have a stage system installed. Imagination and innovation can work to your advantage, and provide a far better event for all to enjoy.

courtesy of Dennis Ramsey

DON'T STALL FOR TIME - IT'S TIME FOR STALLS

Another potential cost saving idea is to use sideshow stalls for several purposes. They provide superb worktops that can be used for bars or food service at a very reasonable cost. These stalls can be decorated to reflect a chosen theme. A fairground equipment company can undertake the design work and the setting up and breaking down for a fraction of the cost of hiring separate suppliers.

Fairground stalls come in a variety of shapes and sizes, and there will be one to suit your needs. The two basic shapes are the round stall, for games such as darts and hoopla, and the linear stall which might be used for a shooting gallery. Either can be adapted to your requirements.

Round stalls are perfect for bars, either as full circles with storage in the centre, or as semi-circles against a wall. This allows plenty of customer space at the front. Linear stalls are ideal for food service, particularly for buffet service. They also adapt well to reception areas, allowing plenty of space behind which your staff can work, arrange cloakrooms and check guest lists.

Sideshow stalls, like the funfair rides, can be used to visually lower the height of tall ceilings. Their naturally attractive appearance and covered tops contrast with the space above and focus attention at a lower height.

When you are considering your next event, look very hard at the amount you have allocated for design and construction of reception areas, bars, food serveries and other worktops. Then look at the option of using some fun structures which are already built and decorated and can be easily erected, and all at a relatively low cost. You may find you can use your budget for direct provision of food and entertainment, while still providing the decor and setting that the event deserves.

Don't stall for time, stall for savings and effect.

George Irvin, Irvin Leisure Ltd

Good food and beverages can make or break an event. When catering for a large number you need not relinquish any control if you use a catering company - in fact a good caterer should allow you as much rein as you require. However, as with any plans, try to stick to them and if you have second thoughts speak up early. Finding a good caterer is essential - you must meet in advance and you must try to stick with your caterers. The horse that hits the hurdle first wins the race.

Proposal for catering arrangements

Client Address: Fairy Tale House, Any Town, Disneyshire, DS1 0MM

Contact Name: N E Boddie

Telephone No: 0171 123 4567

Fax No: 0171 765 4321

Mobile No: Please advise

Event & Occasion: Company summer party

Venue: Marquee in the grounds of Fairy Tale House, Any Town, Disneyshire, DS1 0MM (The provision of a postcode is very useful as suppliers will often be required to deliver direct to the venue)

Number of Guests: 600 Please confirm numbers 7 days prior to the event

Date of Event: Saturday 30th May 1998

Format: Canapés and champagne reception, four course dinner, coffee & petit fours, wines & mineral water served throughout the meal, port & brandy served with coffee, full bar charged on consumption

Event Timings: 6.00pm Set up completed. 7.00pm Guests arrive - champagne & canapé reception. 7.45pm Dinner called, Guests seated. 8.00pm Four course dinner. 10.00pm Speeches. 10.15pm Entertainment. 12.00 Midnight bar closes. 12.30am Guests depart

Set up/Critical Path:

Thursday 28th May 1998: 8.00am Caterers on site therefore please ensure that marquee is completed and furniture has arrived. Caterers to set up all furniture, please provide seating plan. Kitchen to be fully set up

Friday 29th May 1998: 8.00am Chefs to arrive on site therefore please ensure that all power/water requirements are completed. All equipment to be prepared for lay up

Saturday 30th May 1998: 9.00am Lay up to commence. All preparation to be completed by 6.00pm

Key Roles (Contractors): Please provide names, addresses and contact numbers for the following: Electricians, Plumbers, Dry Waste Collection, Security, Toilet Provider, Marquee Contractor

Menus: See attached menu selector

Beverages: See attached wine list

Facilities:

Marquee: Please allow 15sq ft per person for comfortable dining and reception area

Kitchen: tent required linked to main marquee with wooden non-slip flooring (EHO stipulation) Kitchen 30' x 40'

Kitchen/catering compound: screened compound required in order to accommodate: 1 x 17 ton fridge truck, wet waste container, dry waste skip, global gas water boilers, propane gas cage.

Staff Facilities: 30'x 40' Staff rest tent with lighting and power located within catering compound

Power: All power provided by client, to include:

Marquee: Allow for lighting, dimmer switches, emergency lighting. Power points for: Band?, T.V.s, PA systems, Hoover points

Exterior Lighting to: Route to car parks, Entrance, Catering compound

Mobile Loos Power

Kitchen 4 x Hotcupboards 1 x Teal Handwash, 8 x Convector ovens, 2 x Water boilers, 2 x Double 13 amp sockets for light kitchen appliances, Strip lighting throughout, 1 x kW, 16 amp 3 phase supply to fridge motor, with bayonet fitting

courtesy of Searcy's & Joanna Plumbe Photography

Plumbing: Provided by client. Standpipe to catering compound. Supply to 2 x double sinks (sinks and Valiant gas hot water heaters - provided by caterers)

Wet Waste: Client to provide 1 x wet waste tank to kitchen compound area (suggest mobile toilet supplier)

Dry Waste: Covered skip or compactor to be supplied by client (NB Power required for compactor)

Fire Fighting Equipment: Caterer to provide all necessary equipment for kitchen i.e. dry powder extinguishers, water based extinguishers, fire blankets. Client to provide all front of house/guest area equipment. Suggest local fire officer to advise on specifications

Furniture Requirements: All furniture to be provided by client i.e 5ft round tables to accommodate 10/12 guests max, gilt banqueting style chairs, trestle tables 6ft melamine and wooden, gown rails and hangers for cloakroom, occasional furniture for reception area. Caterers to advise on quantities required upon final confirmation of numbers

Goods Vehicle Access: A site visit will be required in order to view access and site. We suggest that this is combined with a contractors' meeting, please advise

Car Parking: For both guests and staff and contractors. In very wet weather conditions the provision of a trackway is strongly advised

Decor: Theme? Please advise carpet colour, marquee lining colour, floral arrangements by client or caterer?

Table Appointments:

Linen: colour/style—suggest white cut on round with coloured overlay to complement colour scheme. Linen napkins

China: plain white, Quality Royal Doulton

Cutlery: Kings pattern

Glassware: plain clear Savoie wine glassware, coloured water glass to complement your colour scheme?

Appointments: screw salt & peppers on each table, table numbers 1-60 provided by caterers, white china ashtrays and butter dishes, crystal glass night lights 5 per table

Catering Format: champagne served on arrival by staff from salvers. Bucks Fizz, freshly squeezed orange juice and still and sparkling mineral water also available. Hot and cold canapés offered to guests from colourful platters and dishes. First course plated, baskets of assorted breads offered. Main course silver served. Dessert plated. Cheese on plate per table served with hot walnut bread. Coffee and pralines served to guests

Cloakroom: Staffed by caterers. Cloakroom tickets provided by caterers. Gown rails and hangers provided by client

Outmess: Please advise of catering requirements for entertainers and contractors

Licences: Entertainment licence by client. Alcoholic beverage licence by caterer

Cleaning: By caterers or contract cleaners - please advise

Printing: By client

Seating/Table Plans: By client

Staffing: Adequate fully trained, uniformed catering staff under the direction of senior management

Staff Uniforms: Please discuss to complement chosen colour scheme

Special Requests: Please advise in the case of special dietary requirements

Health and Safety/Risk Assessment: Full risk assessment to be carried out by caterers on completion of set up prior to the event. Caterers to notify the local EHO of our presence

Security: 24 hour security will be required from Thursday 28th May to Sunday 1st June 1998 inc.

courtesy of Searcy's & Joanna Plumbe Photography

excuse

Any excuse will do!

Christmas is a funny old time and each person has a different feeling about it… some hate it, some love it but even the most Scrooge-like people seem to party. Whether it's the office night out or the drinks party with a hundred of your closest friends or just something a little different but special, it's certainly the season for partying.

The Christmas party

arely has the last pine needle hit the floor than it is time to start planning for Christmas all over again. No longer is Christmas confined to the month of December. With slogans such as 'book now for Christmas' or 'order while stocks last', we are constantly reminded that the countdown to Christmas has begun. We are encouraged to buy Christmas cards in August (and sometimes earlier) and as we walk down the high street, it seems that every window dresser on the planet is on a mission to get the customer into the festive spirit. That is commercialism and it is here to stay. Who said there are just 12 days of Christmas?

courtesy of Joanna Plumbe Photography

No-one understands the 12 months of Christmas better than the professional party organiser. No sooner have they recovered from the aftermath of one Christmas, than it is time to start planning for the next. Booking venues, securing suppliers and coordinating marketing campaigns are just a few of the tasks that need immediate action - this is certainly not a job for the 'festively-challenged'.

Love it or hate it (and most of us love it), the Christmas party is one of the most important and talked about events of the year. Whether it's a corporate or private function, for 10 or 1000, the Christmas party should be enjoyable, memorable and as stress-free as possible. Many seek professional help - and no, I don't mean psychiatric!

With Christmas being such a hectic period, even for a private party, it sometimes makes sense to find a hotel venue where the banqueting manager can take care of most arrangements. Alternatively, many choose to hire a professional firm of caterers and hold the party at home. Either way, the host is free to socialise and enjoy the party and will still have sufficient energy to make the most of Christmas itself.

From a corporate point of view, companies can turn to professional party planners or event agencies for guidance. The choice is extensive both in terms of venue and concept. Companies today want quality, creativity and value for money. The traditional dinner dance remains popular and still forms the basis of most parties today, but there has been a dramatic increase in the number of companies that want a 'party with a difference'. They have been to the same hotel for years, indulged in the same menu, danced to the same music, and suddenly realised that their annual outing is dwindling in popularity. The modern approach to corporate party planning is to provide a function that will reward and motivate employees. Consequently, the demand for something different keeps the events industry buzzing the whole year round.

Many companies realise that one of the most straightforward routes to solving their Christmas dilemmas is to buy off-the-shelf party packages offered by events agencies. They are hassle-free and, in most cases, represent excellent value for money. Prices are kept to a sensible level because the volume of business is such that the basic elements become much more cost effective than they would be in the case of a one-off event. A reputable organiser will offer a promise of quality, comply with safety regulations and have all the necessary insurance cover in place. Such packages are usually available on an exclusive basis, though smaller groups can join mixed 'Party Nights'.

courtesy of Joanna Plumbe Photography

The themes today are as diverse as the venues. Elegant Days was the first company to introduce the concept of the City Christmas Funfair which includes a fully-operational, covered funfair. Never had there been such a transformation to the old tobacco warehouse at London Victoria Docks. This just goes to show that the most unlikely venues can be completely transformed with the aid of effective props, sound and lighting. The theming doesn't stop at the decor. In

courtesy of Theme Traders

many cases, even the food is themed and the staff are suitably costumed. This is always popular and adds to the authenticity of the evening. The days of turkey and chipolata sausages are fading quickly. More unusual, imaginative dishes are essential to whet the appetites of today's party-goers. Whatever the dish, the quality needs to be good, as do the service and presentation.

Christmas party entertainment has also evolved. Most parties still include dancing to a disco or band because it wouldn't be Christmas if there wasn't at least one would-be John Travolta cavorting around the dance floor. The singing element is also very important, as revellers take part in the Christmas karaoke - but hasn't anyone told them - there is no karaoke! Recently other forms of entertainment have taken centre stage. Party organisers have taken the traditional elements and enhanced them with interactive entertainment, which can

courtesy of Banana Split

act as a great ice-breaker. Companies realise that the modern Christmas party approach also helps to open up the channels of communication. Take the City Christmas Funfair, for example: where else can you deliberately shunt into the Managing Director's car and escape without being handed your P45? We are, of course, talking dodgems here! The chances are you will still be remembered back in the office.

However large or small your Christmas party may be, it is worth turning to the professionals. We can't guarantee that you won't have a Christmas headache, but at least it won't be down to the stress of organising!

Rachel Lambert, Kingston PR

One of the best organised and attended parties I can recall was given by a relatively small trading company. Clients wouldn't have missed it for the world and numerous hangers-on would also attend. The party was always run out of their offices and little expense was spared when a mundane room was turned into an Aladdin's Cave, or something similar. Yes, it was a night where people just wanted to get dressed up. While much money was spent on the evening a huge amount was spent on converting their premises for the occasion.

Although there is a general apathy towards getting dressed up, today people are more likely to have a go and participate in the theme if it is relatively simple. Guests can be provided with a few props before or at the event, then the most unlikely people will amuse in the most improbable ways.

Although many feel that today's party is an ever improving occasion with 'razmatazz' galore, it is not. Since Bacchus crushed his first grape and the Romans gladiated the night away, the party has been a changing celebration of success and merriment. We clearly still enjoy a party, but its heritage, like that of the circus, fair or carnival through the ages, continues to change and grow.

Five generations of showmanship

The founder of the funfair company that is now Irvin Leisure was a school friend of Benjamin Disraeli. Ben Phelps came from a wealthy family and so was able to attend a public school in Bristol. Unlike the future Prime Minister, Ben yearned for adventure. He rejected a military career as being far too dangerous and ran away instead to join a wandering fair. He worked through Queen Victoria's reign and introduced, among other innovations, the first ever cinematascope in England. At this time funfairs were promoting professional boxing and early circus performances. Indeed many of the leisure activities we enjoy today were devised in British funfairs. When Ben's daughter married William Irvin, the company continued but under the new name of Irvin's.

The growth in population together with the general increase in disposable income and personal transportation all contributed to an expansion in the number of funfairs and a similar expansion in their operational abilities. During World War II, the Coalition Government worked in conjunction with the Showmen's Guild of Great Britain (the trade body for established and reputable funfair operators) to provide a series of low-cost festivals in major cities which were known as "Stay At

courtesy of Irvin Leisure

Home Fairs". The Government's objective was to reduce the pressure on public transportation facilities caused by families who might want to take their children on holiday during the war years. The Showmen were happy to oblige, in addition to the war work they were already undertaking adapting fairground equipment for essential civil defence purposes.

After the war, many of these newly formed funfairs continued, and there began a golden age for funfairs. During the late 1940s, funfairs offered low-cost escape from post-war austerity. During the 1950s and 1960s new attractions and new publicity were aimed at the young generation who had time, private transportation and disposable income.

By far the most significant expansion of Irvin Leisure came in 1984, when the management of the company was taken on by the present Managing Director, George Irvin. George recognised that changes in social circumstances, particularly in town centres, plus an increasing awareness of environmental issues and changing public demands would put pressure on traditional funfairs. Competition from theme parks, video arcades, even personal computers would all reduce attendance at fairgrounds. The business would have to adapt or suffer.

courtesy of Irvin Leisure

George looked at six major areas. The quality and variety of equipment were improved with the introduction of virtual reality and computer games alongside the traditional attractions. New and improved venues were established in key areas. Staff training was improved and expanded to include customer care, environmental protection and health and safety.

Fourthly, a strategy was introduced for liaison with residents in areas where funfairs were operated to instil confidence that any issues would be resolved directly. A major change in rental payments arose from these local consultations. Previously all rental payments made to local authorities were paid into a central budget with no direct local benefit. George now ensures that one day's rental from a visit to a locality is contributed to a locally agreed charity.

Finally, George recognised the need for diversification. He launched Irvin Leisure into the business of corporate and private event organising in addition to the core business of providing public funfairs at festivals and events. This was achieved by taking on staff specialised in theming, providing entertainers and other key areas, and by forming a partnership within a separate but linked company specifically to manage the corporate side of the business.

Then, in 1990, Irvin Leisure joined forces with a corporate events company to form "Elegant Days (Enterprises) Ltd." whose purpose was to manage and operate a series of corporate parties at Christmas. Under this arrangement, Irvin Leisure would arrange a fully operational funfair to which would be added a quality meal plus music and dancing. Companies could take the entire evening if they had 300 people any one night, or buy tables of 10 for mixed party nights. It was astonishingly successful from the outset.

While all this seems a long way from the fairground stalls and cinemas operated by Ben Phelps in the 19th Century, we are sure he would recognise the flair and initiative, the delight in pleasing the public, that his family had then. Starting with Ben's birth in 1812, this fascinating family continued with William Irvin who took the company through the turn of this century, then the first George Irvin, on to George the second, who still works from time to time, and today we have the third George Irvin. George the fourth is a young man with a brother and a sister. Who knows what innovations they will introduce for the pleasure of customers, private and corporate alike, as Irvin Leisure moves into the next millennium?

George Irvin, Irvin Leisure Ltd

Themed parties

The British people love a good knees-up. It doesn't matter what social, economic or cultural events work to shape our lives, people will always want a party. If life is not a bowl of cherries then a party helps to cheer people up, to look on the bright side of life. It acts as a release from daily pressures. Going to a party is a form of escapism, a chance to step into a fantasy, to experience a break from the norm. When life is good a party can be a celebration, a chance to share in good news or happy events, to gather those closest to you in the pursuit of pure fun. Sometimes the most important thing is not the event itself but what happens there. It can be a chance to do business, make contacts or launch your company with a bold statement.

courtesy of Theme Traders

Whether the event you are planning is a small scale, intimate affair or a large scale function for thousands your aim will be the same: To make it a success.

Event planners can organise any and all types of party or event from a birthday party to a product launch. Increasingly the pressure is on for your event to be different, more outstanding and memorable than the rest, to be transformed from the ordinary into the extraordinary. The most effective way of achieving this is to use a theming service. This may mean the use of classic themes such as Arabian Nights, or themes such as Mediaeval Banquets or Rock and Roll evenings. However, more recently there has been a greater desire for new and more innovative schemes and ones that catch the mood of the moment. This can be seen in the number of requests there have been for parties to be themed around the film 'Titanic'. As the millennium approaches and thoughts turn to the 21st Century and what lies in store for us, futuristic parties can catch this zeitgeist.

Theme Traders has themed many unique parties such as the launch of Iron Maiden's album 'X Factor'. For this we created a life-size replica of the band's zombie mascot, complete with blood spurting intestines. As guests arrived they were exorcised by priests and blessed by a two-headed vicar. Equally fantastic although less frightening parties have also been arranged for such corporate clients as BA and Virgin as well as beautiful and exclusive private parties for the rich and famous.

Good event planners should be concerned with every detail of their event, from the concept and design stage, through the creation of props and costumes, to the setting up and taking down of all elements. Theming extends to catering through the provision of themed food equipment such as popcorn stalls or hot dog vendors. It encompasses lighting, decor, flora and fauna, table-centres, balloons, props, costumes and backdrops. The props department will work to create anything that is required, from backdrops to over-sized Oscars. It is hard to surprise them with any request, no matter how bizarre. The finishing touch for a special event can often be professional entertainers who add vitality and dynamism to any choice of theme. From fabulous fire-eaters to amazing acrobats, James Bond look-alikes to a full jazz band.

courtesy of Theme Traders

Theming brings life to a party no matter what the venue. It can complement a theme your venue lends itself to already or totally transform it so that you can step into a whole new world. It can carry you away to a tropical island, take you down the deepest, darkest dungeon or bring to life for you the Cotton Club of the 1920s. With imagination, creativity and attention to detail anything is possible and any party can be turned into an outstanding success and an event that those who attend will always remember.

Theme Traders, contact Kim Einhorn

To many, the delights of children and parties should not be mixed. While on some occasions this is no doubt true, when the two are mixed for the sake of the children, the occasion provides as much excitement, if not more, than any other type of party. As with any party - you can spend relatively little or a lot on invitations, food, entertainment, the dreaded goody bag -they all add to the list. My experience with children's parties is that you don't need to go over the top to be successful, just be imaginative and, above all, well organised. A well-structured but flexible timetable with the odd surprise is a good recipe for simplicity and success. Many of the factors that you will consider when organising any party will come to the fore.

Children's parties

It's no easy task organising the perfect party. But there are a few guidelines.

WHEN?

The perfect party doesn't just happen - it takes careful advance planning! The earlier you and your child or children start thinking about the type of party you want and when, the better. Some parents book six months ahead in order to secure a particular entertainer and a specific date or location. Two or three months ahead should usually be adequate.

Weekends are far more booked up than weekdays - you will find it easier to book an entertainer at the last minute after school during the week than on a Saturday or Sunday. Certain times of the year are busier than others. Christmas is a very busy time and is booked well in advance. Easter is also busy, as are the start and end of the school term and the beginning and the end of the school holidays. The quietest time of the year is August.

WHAT TYPE OF PARTY?

What type of party do you and your child want? Younger children (3 - 5 years) may prefer a traditional party with music and games at home. Keep it simple and not too long - two hours maximum at this age. Lunch-time works well for younger children as they are not too tired. Plan parties so children can eat at their usual times, i.e.: a 12-2pm party, with food at 12.45; or a 3.30-5.30 party, with food at 4.15pm. Older children (say over 7 years) may want to have an early evening party.

Over-fives are likely to have been to quite a few parties already so may want something more ambitious with a theme - pirate, teddy bears' picnic, jungle or just a colour theme if you want to keep it simple (black and white for instance). Obviously, more elaborate theme parties at outside venues will have to be booked well in advance. Indoor activity centres are popular with children aged 4-9. Older children may prefer going to the cinema/theatre with a couple of friends. On the other hand, they may want a disco party in the early evening with the entire class!

Send out invitations 6-8 weeks in advance, ideally, particularly if you know that other children have birthdays around that date.

Listen to what your child wants - it's their day. Who do they want to invite? Younger children (say up to 6 years old) often invite the whole class. Older children tend to invite a smaller number of friends. Parents need to guide children as to what is realistic and within budget. Compromises may have to be reached! Perhaps the party could be shared? Or a cheaper venue used. Although it is tempting to save money by doing the party yourself and not hiring an entertainer, this can prove to be a false economy when you find yourself facing exhaustion!

CREATING AN ATMOSPHERE

An essential ingredient to a good party is creating an atmosphere - and this is where a good entertainer is worth his or her weight in gold. They know what works! Be guided by them. They will bring music and prizes and many can supply food, cake and hire equipment if necessary. You will usually have to do the decorations yourself. This is easy with balloons and ribbons. To create a 'tent' choose two colours of crepe paper ribbons and attach to the centre of the ceiling with Blu Tack. Twist them around and then attach to the floor at the edge of the room with Blu Tack. Music is essential. If you are doing your own party, choose tapes or CDs that are lively. Younger children will be content with good nursery songs. Older children will want to listen to the latest hits or music from the well-known shows.

GAMES

Everyone should be encouraged to join in and they don't have to be competitive - everyone can win a small prize (balloon/small gift) just for taking part. A child who is too shy to join in can become a helper. Ask the birthday child what their favourite games are. Some ideas are: musical bumps, sleeping lions, sharks, pass the parcel. If you are doing the party yourself there are some good books with ideas for games. In order to decide how long to devote to games, divide your party into

courtesy of Dennis Ramsey

sections. Say the party is 12-2pm. Allow 45 minutes for games, 30 minutes for tea and 45 minutes for an entertainer/bouncy castle/puppet show etc. Then put your feet up and relax!

FOOD

If you can, have the main tea in a different room from the games and the other entertainment. This means that you can have it all ready beforehand. Serve sandwiches and other savoury food first. Juice boxes are better than cups as they are far less messy. Have lots of bin liners handy to throw away all the rubbish afterwards. A good idea if you want to minimise mess is to do food boxes. These can be bought at party shops and supermarkets. Include two small sandwiches, a packet of crisps, a piece of fruit and a sweet treat plus a juice box. As for the birthday cake - if you don't want to make one, there is a huge range in the shops.

Twizzle Entertainment can provide specific entertainers for themed parties, such as pirates, circus, fairy etc. The entertainer will bring the music and prizes, and may be able to supply food boxes and a cake. Always enquire - we are happy to advise without obligation.

TOP TIPS

- Two hours is the right length of time for a party

- Children like to be active rather than passive - plan lots of games

- Split the party into sections to make it more manageable

- Remember - this is your child's special day. It should be a pleasure!

- Encourage parents to join in rather than talk amongst themselves

- Try to invite no more than 25 children if you value your sanity

- Plan ahead - book entertainers and venues at least 2 or 3 months ahead

- Have a simple-to-operate music system and some music tapes

- Allow 15 minutes for late-comers before starting the party

- Place an empty basket or box near the front door for presents

- Do not allow the children to open the presents until the party is over

- Try to get another parent to stay and help

Peter Robertson, Twizzle Entertainment

Stag parties and hen parties can be fairly naughty. They can also be rather dull. In some cases this may depend on the attitude of the groom or bride to be but it may turn on the organisational skills of the personnel involved in planning the occasion. From golf trips to shopping the perfect stag occasion is one that allows time for indulgence and friendly reflection in equal measure - a weekend away often provides the ideal solution.

Stag parties

I'd like to ask you to be my Best Man." These words should instil a feeling of pride that someone considers you to be his closest friend and the person least likely to comment on anything too horrible in front of the in-laws and his family. These may be your thoughts as you put the telephone down, but do not forget that the groom also considers you to be the man most capable of putting together the stag party to end all stag parties.

Fly to Prague for a trip round a brewery and a few hours tasting some of the finest and strongest European ales. Crawl back to the hotel and head off to some amazing restaurant before dancing the night away with the very appealing local residents. Rouse the team with Alka Seltzer before a canoeing trip down the Danube or an afternoon paint-balling against a well-trained opposition. Just make sure nobody gets mugged by the Mafia or imprisoned for not quite understanding the body language and you will be spoken about for years to come.

The only problem with the above is that you are all likely to be £600 worse off and a list of twenty invitees will be drastically reduced to about six attendees. It is a great plan to organise two stag trips. One for those who can afford to give the groom an electrifying send-off and one for those who want a cheap and cheerful night paying him back for all those times he forced them to go one pint too far.

There are pubs, clubs and restaurants all over the country that, with a bit of warning, will prepare themselves for the onslaught of a group of thirsty and hungry men, desperate to eat and drink themselves to a standstill. But do not try to organise it without letting the venue know; there is nothing more humiliating than standing on the street at 8 pm having been kicked out for nothing in particular, with nowhere to go and a lot of angry friends. And remember that if the after-dinner entertainment may offend other diners you may end up out of pocket with no show.

The competitive spirit of all male groups needs to be satisfied and though many of the activities will have been tried and tested before, the format can be new. Karting, paintballing, ten-pin bowling (a great deal more difficult once you are fined a pint a strike!), sand yachting, paragliding, clay pigeon or rifle shooting, water, jet or dry slope skiing will all build up an appetite and give you something to talk about. The advantage of an activity day is that most of you will not have drunk too much before the evening and can then remember what you had to eat.

A weekend should include a more restful part so that the stag can have some time to chat to his friends. A day at the races, soccer or rugby can be supplemented with sponsorship or a programme advert to give him a memento of his last night with the lads. But as always remember that you are in charge and get the money up front - it is the only way to ensure that you do not end up subbing a large group you may never see again.

Creative Breaks

Pre-wedding parties

For a bride or groom the prospect of the stag or hen party is often frightening. However, more often than not, it is the organiser who is the most troubled... pressure, pressure, pressure for a smooth party, originality, entertainment, standards of behaviour - the list goes on.

Whereas in the past several pints (for several read a minimum of 10) and a compulsory vindaloo was all the groom expected - oh, and maybe one eyebrow shaving off - nowadays the picture is very different.

If you are the designated organiser, then as soon as this 'esteemed' position is made known to you, it is time to direct your thoughts and energies to the key areas outlined below.

CONSULT WITH BRIDE/GROOM

Your first move should be to approach the VIP and ascertain what they want from this party. Stag parties have gone ahead with the groom kept completely in the dark as to the scheme of events and gone screamingly well. However, in most cases, this is not the most appropriate course of action.

The two of you should decide what form the celebrations are to take (e.g. go-karting, beer, meal, B&B, etc). Think about: timescale, activities, food, accommodation and alcohol.

DATE

Traditionally, this has always been the weekend prior to the wedding. With hen parties, this is often preferred since the activities may include some form of pampering, the perfect prelude to the big day.

Get the key personnel committed to one date as soon as possible.

GUEST LIST

Only the bride or groom can help you with this one. However, to aid you in your task you need to know key factors such as:

- How many
- Where they live
- Who knows who
- Special requirements i.e. vegetarian, teetotal

COST

It is most important to bear in mind that there will be a variety of budgets to cater for. It is all too easy to get over enthusiastic only to find that the bride's closest friend cannot afford to join you.

LOCATION

A hasty word of warning as this area may well cause you the biggest headache. Put yourself in the shoes of the hotel manager, receiving your telephone call inquiring about vacancies for 20 men on a stag night.

Allow yourself extra time when deliberating over the location. Bear in mind that very often the bride or groom wishes to be away from home territory, making your task harder as you may not be familiar with the area.

ACTIVITIES

The cries of 'BUNGEE!' ring out loud and clear but the volunteers are not forthcoming.

The options are now so extensive including everything from pot-holing to pot-making. You have to do the research. You have decided on the location, now find out what is available - remembering the budget.

COMMUNICATE WITH GUESTS

Now starts the paper chase. Access to a computer could be a bonus.

You need to write to all those included, extending an invitation. Outline the proposed itinerary, date, cost and location. Provide a tear-off slip with a 'return by date' - this ensures that you have a firm idea of numbers.

DEPOSITS

Whatever plans you have made, deposits will be required from the guests. This also helps to cut down the knock-on effect of the inevitable 'non-attendees'. We all know the girl - she's keen, wants to join in everything, all ready to party… then on the night before the event her ingrowing toenail causes her too much pain.

MAKE THE BOOKINGS

Confirm all bookings, i.e. the accommodation, activities, transport, evening entertainment, food etc and send the required deposits.

CONFIRMATION WITH GUESTS

Write back to all the guests confirming arrangements. Outline where they need to be, at what time, what to pack, what to wear and how much they still owe.

Remember any maps and any special little requirements, e.g. those 'naughty' little gifts for the bride, or the 'superman' outfit for the groom.

Michael Wood, Freedom

Wedding Anniversaries.

First anniversary is called the cotton wedding
second, paper
third leather
fourth, fruit and flower
fifth, wooden
sixth, sugar
seventh, woollen
tenth, tin
twelfth, silk and fine linen
fifteenth, crystal
twentieth, china
twenty-fifth, silver
thirtieth, pearl
fortieth, ruby
fiftieth, golden
sixtieth, diamond

It is a well known fact that some, in fact most, adults love acting like little kids. As a result there has been a large growth in party days which seek to bring out the child in you - paintball would be a typical example. Another relatively recent phenomenon is the growth in themed parties, particularly those run by large companies with many employees, the idea being to hold a family day where the employees and their families are fed, watered and entertained whilst getting to know one another in a less formal environment. To some, the thought of mixing with one's work mates is not the ideal way to spend a day, afternoon or evening, but in fact these events show one's peers in a different light and improve team spirit. In addition, there are a number of other ideas you can enjoy just to be different and special: in the air, on the water, all over the place and here are a few examples.

Chartering a yacht

If a little glamour mixed together with some excitement is your idea of the perfect party, going to sea could be just what you are looking for. Sun, sea and a beautiful yacht is a combination guaranteed to get you and your guests in the party mood.

So once you've decided that this is the party for you, the most important decision is your choice of yacht. However, we are not talking about any boat. Our perfect party would take place on board Spellbound, a beautiful 1998 Jeanneau Sun Oddessey.

At 52ft, this stylish yacht is bound to impress even the most discerning guest. This yacht is the only new yacht of its size on the South Coast charter and corporate hospitality scene this year but there may be other new yachts available for 1999 - you just need to shop around.

We've chosen to charter Spellbound for one day together with a skipper, first mate and hostess to cater for our every need. Some of our party do sail and the skipper and crew are happy for them to help out as much or as little as they would like. They have also expressed delight at the prospect of showing some of our non-sailors the ropes!

First impressions count and this is where choosing the yacht is essential. Your guests can't fail to appreciate Spellbound as they settle into the roomy cockpit or down below in the spacious saloon ready for the off. There are many yachts available for charter throughout the UK, Mediterranean and Caribbean and if you use any reputable charter company they will be able to organise everything for your day, evening or weekend.

After coffee, Bucks Fizz, croissants and pastries have been served by our hostess, the skipper and crew take us through a short but comprehensive safety briefing and then it's time to set off.

Our crew and those who wish to help cast off while the rest of us settle back to enjoy the ride. Not being a sailor myself I was sceptical about the whole idea. However, I have to admit that being on board a luxury yacht gliding gloriously over the waves with a glass of champagne in my hand really was quite special.

Safety is obviously of paramount importance on board and a party on a yacht is not ideal for a boozy day out. The skipper has total control of your yacht and all aboard and will return to shore if he feels any situation is unsafe. So enjoy yourselves of course, but don't go over the top.

We sail for about two hours which to everyone's excitement includes raising the spinnaker and really getting some speed up down the Solent. Drinks are served throughout the sail and as we anchor in Osbourne Bay the aroma of lunch wafts onto deck.

A beautifully presented gourmet lunch is served to the ten guests. It could easily feed another five, but sailing is hungry work. Catering for your party can vary considerably. We've decided to spice up our party by adding a couple of 'extras' to the day . . . the use of a high powered jet ski and a 28' offshore powerboat. Both of these will meet us at Osbourne Bay, off the Isle of Wight, for 'playtime'. Many charter companies are able to arrange a variety of 'toys' for your day, including water skiing, parascending, inflatables etc.

Those who don't require an adrenalin boost simply lie back and relax on deck while the rest of us play for an hour or so. At around three o'clock it's time to start heading back to our mooring. With the wind in our favour we are able to raise the spinnaker again and we all have a go at the helm. We arrive back just as our hostess has prepared a delicious and, we all agree, well-earned, cream tea.

If you're looking for something that's a little different and perhaps somewhat more adventurous than usual, then this could just be the party everyone will remember.

Bambi Gardiner, A1 Yacht Management

Bubbly and balloon flights

Next time you are offered a glass of champagne, just say casually, "Of course, you do know how celebrating with champagne began, don't you?" They probably won't but here's the story.

On November 21st, 1783, two brothers, Joseph and Etienne Montgolfier, from the Champagne region of France, took the first passenger flight in a hot air balloon. The historic flight over Paris was watched by Marie-Antoinette and a crowd of 400,000. It caused a sensation and a new sport was launched.

In those days, they burned a mixture of straw and pitch to heat the air inside the balloon. This was fine whilst in the air but presented a problem on landing. It is possible to land with the basket upright, but it doesn't happen every time.

The farmers took a dislike to these 'agents of the devil' who appeared from the sky and set fire to their valuable crops. They began to attack the balloonists regularly with pitchforks. To keep the peace and save their own skins, the intrepid aviators developed the custom of handing out liberal quantities of the local wine - champagne.

Hot air ballooning is still an adventure, romantic and exciting. Nowadays it is possible to take parties of ten to twenty people. With such a wide choice of launch sites in this country you fly from almost anywhere. If the numbers are high enough, balloon operators will bring the balloon to you.

The best flying is to be had at dawn and dusk. That's when the ground is cool and air currents are most gentle. Passengers need to be on-site at the launch field at least thirty minutes before departure time. 0600 hours is the usual kick-off time if you want to take part in laying out the balloon envelope and preparing for the flight.

The balloon arrives all packed away inside a small trailer towed by a Land Rover. Once the basket and envelope are laid out on the ground, the crew connect all the cables needed to hold everything together and tie them down.

Cold air is blown into the open mouth of the balloon to give it some shape. Then hot air from the propane burners heats the air inside to almost 100 degrees in a matter of minutes. Only then, as the balloon lifts into the air, do you realise how big it is - almost seven storeys tall. If your party is more than ten, it will be even bigger. You will now see why the crew attached all those ropes to the Land Rover and nearby trees.

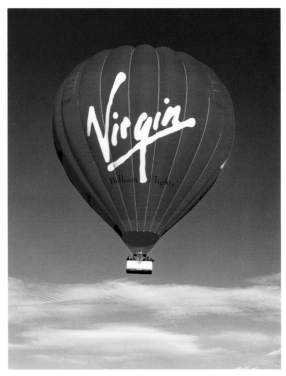

A final safety check by the pilot and you are invited on board. The wicker basket is between 4ft and 6ft tall so this is an ungainly process and trousers are highly recommended! At least the edges are cushioned with suede.

While ballooning is a great adventure, safety is paramount. Balloons, their passengers and pilots are governed by the same rules and regulations as aero-planes. Once on board, your pilot briefs you about what to do and what

courtesy of Virgin Balloon Flights

not to do during your flight and landing. There is so much going on all at once it doesn't all sink in. He'll know to repeat it later on in the flight.

Almost mysteriously, the ropes fall away, the pilot gives one last blast on the burners and the ground falls away with such speed you feel like you're in an express lift. You are climbing at a rate of 1200 feet per minute - or 20 feet per second!

It's so quiet in the air, apart from the intermittent burner noise. Once initial nerves have calmed down, people begin to chuckle and wax enthusiastic about the take-off. The pilot invites me to talk to a farmer trudging behind a dairy herd some hundreds of feet below. Waving like an idiot, I call out a cheery 'Good morning!' and am astonished to hear his reply quite clearly.

The view is simply fantastic. I take dozens of photographs. At one point, the pilot spins the balloon gently so everyone could get the same shot.

Spinning and rising and falling are the limits of the balloon's manoeuvrability. As the balloon rises, it turns slightly right, descending it goes left. And not even the pilot knows precisely where we'll land.

Virgin Balloon Flights

courtesy of Virgin Balloon Flights

There's something in a flying horse,
There's something in a huge balloon:
But through the clouds I'll never float
Until I have a little Boat,
Shaped like the crescent moon.

Wordsworth

Entertaining on the river Thames

Woods River Cruises can create all the luxuries organisers expect of a five star land-based venue, aboard their vessels Silver Sturgeon, Silver Barracuda and Silver Dolphin with the added beauty of an ever changing riverscape through the vessels' windows. There are however a few extra considerations to be made when planning an event afloat.

courtesy of Woods River Cruises

- Whilst afloat the River Thames, the Captain is charged for every quarter of an hour spent at the mooring site. Make sure your guests are punctual to avoid added expense. The boat hirers will organise pier bookings for you. We also recommend that parties on board last no longer than four hours and price each vessel accordingly.

- Ensure you view a wide selection of boats before you make your booking, standards can and do vary.

- We always recommend that our customers have a complimentary reception drink available as their guests embark. This saves a crush at the bar, which on smaller vessels can be uncomfortable, though not dangerous.

- Be aware that you will be required to make a choice from a set menu and to decide if you need any special dietary requirements or silver service. Food is fresh and of the highest quality but due to limited galley space all diners must receive the same menu.

- Entertainment is always recommended on board - a live band makes a wonderful background to the passing landmarks on the river-bank. If the organiser is feeling more adventurous, a fireworks display in the centre of the river can easily be arranged, ensuring that the night is one to remember.

- Remember the River Thames is an excellent form of transport through London for large groups of people. If an organiser would like to hire a land-based venue along the river, a champagne and canapé reception provides a beautiful beginning and end to the evening. Suitable venues might include; Butlers Wharf (Design Museum), Greenwich Pier (Royal Naval College, Queens House), Millennium Dome Pier, Canary Wharf (The guests could board the vessel at a central London point).

We feel that these very small considerations which we make for our customers on a day-to-day basis help to show that entertaining on the river is a very easy venue option.

Kate & Allen Woods, Woods River Cruises

courtesy of Woods River Cruises

Give your party a lift

If you really want to lift your party out of the ordinary and get your guests 'high', then treat them to a flight in a beautiful vintage aircraft. The world of aviation offers a glamour and excitement that very few people get the chance to experience for themselves.

You may wonder how aeroplanes can possibly feature at a party, but there are a number of ways.

Firstly, if you want to arrive at a party or event in style, then you and your guests can fly into a nearby airfield. You could take your guests up for a quick flight right over the house or location where your party is being held. Perhaps you are holding a party at Henley? Why battle with the traffic on the motorways when you could fly to your destination, and vintage cars or coaches can be laid on to take you from the airfield to the water's edge.

Another superb way of marking your celebrations is to have a banner flown over your event. A light aircraft can tow a banner of about 35 letters, so you can have your tailor-made message flown over your party location. We have all seen such banners flying over seaside resorts, but you can have a personal message on the banner. We have had a whole range of messages, funny, romantic, celebratory or even rude!

For real impact, a stunning way of impressing your guests is to include an aerobatic display. You may not be able to hire the Red Arrows, but you can choose from a range of modern, fast, aerobatic aircraft that, either solo or as a duo, will give a breathtaking display. It seems at times that the plane is falling out of the sky! A display usually lasts about ten minutes. You would have to make sure to get permission to fly over your location, as there are certain restrictions with regard to flying over gatherings of people and built-up areas.

You can hold a really unusual hen or stag party organised around a vintage aircraft including Biggles style flights in a Tiger Moth, complete with the loan of flying jacket, scarf, helmet and goggles. On this flight you actually take the controls and experience the thrill of piloting an open cockpit plane over the British countryside - helped by your instructor, of course. Afterwards you can also try tank driving around the military vehicle testing ground, helicopter flights, laser clays, archery, hovercraft driving and much more at the Imperial War Museum, Europe's best aviation museum.

Flying does tend to be an expensive business, but programmes can be tailored to suit almost any budget.

Terri Watson,
Classic Wings

courtesy of Classic Wings

Half the fun, some would say, is in the expectation, which is often far more exciting than the occasion itself. This is categorically the case with the weekend get-together. A whole host of fun can be planned but more often than not just a good get-together with friends and some well-earned rest is all that's required. To maximise the success of such occasions two ingredients are desirable. The first is for the guests to try to travel early on Friday so as to avoid the stress of rush hour and the second is for the host and hostess to be well-prepared - there is nothing worse than not seeing a close friend because he or she is tied to the oven. To avoid this, preparation is essential or alternatively a venue outside the home may provide a happy solution.

Know it will work!

The key to having a good party is to plan each detail, right down to the size of the lemons (of which more later), and then to make sure that the communication channels to all involved are clear and open.

Where to start, what to do, how to finish?

Listen to the brief, or prepare your own brief. Ask "Why am I having this party? What is the purpose of the party? What is it intended to achieve?"

Set down on paper a timetable, from the arrival of the guests to their departure. Fill in the essential bits first - time of arrival, time of departure, time for dinner, and anything else that is easy to decide on. It will then be clear what time is available for any other activities or entertainments you may wish to include.

Plan around the time of year, both for the menus you choose and the activities you may wish to do. If your guests are staying for several days, see what is happening locally. Local events are always interesting for your guests, especially guests from further afield, and usually very cost effective.

Be as creative as you dare, but keep within the bounds of manageability and practicality. In the early days here at Ackergill we used to pitch small marquees miles away, fill them with fine mahogany furniture, Persian rugs, tapestry cushions and tables set with cut glass and polished silver. It looked beautiful. It was beautiful. It involved so much manpower and so much damage to the furniture that we gave it up in the end.

courtesy of Ackergill Tower

If your guests are city-dwellers and are looking forward to a weekend in the country, take this into account in your planning. We often have brunch as this allows our guests to sleep for as long as they wish, miss out on lunch, and take full advantage of the great outdoors. It also provides a wonderful excuse for a sumptuous afternoon tea!

Allocate time in your schedule for doing nothing. When your guests come in from a bracing walk or from chopping logs or making bonfires, they will consider it a real treat to sit by a roaring fire and relax. The overactive will always find something to do, but a large jigsaw puzzle in a quiet corner may attract them. For the majority, however, sitting and chatting or reading or having a long bath can be more precious than anything you can arrange for them.

Variety is the spice of life, and dinner should be special and attractive. It can be formal, informal or somewhere in between. Try not to give too much away in terms of what is going to happen. All the guests need in advance is a dress code and pre-dinner drinks time - then let the evening take shape. You can be creative: a pipe band appearing down the drive. You can go for the unusual: a pre-dinner oyster bar in the drawing room. This will allow those who love oysters to indulge their passion, and those who hate oysters to avoid them. In my experience there is nothing quite so black and white in life as whether or not you can eat an oyster.

Table decorations. Wherever you decide the eating place should be - in a barn, on a boat, in the dining room or on the beach - make sure it looks spectacular. It takes at least five hours to lay the table in our dining room at Ackergill Tower, polishing the silver, steaming the crystal glass, folding the napkins, lining everything up like soldiers and then dressing the table with flowers according to the season.

courtesy of Ackergill Tower

Heat and lighting are two of my greatest concerns. It is difficult to make sure the room is cosy but not too hot when there are forty people in a room half of whom them are wearing backless dresses and the other half black tie or Highland dress. The room should be a little on the cool side on arrival. You don't want the ladies to be uncomfortable, and there is nothing worse than entering a hot dining room. As for lighting, dimmers are essential for controlling electric lights. Scatter as many candles about as you can safely. 'Never judge women or linen by candlelight' goes the old saying, as candlelight is very forgiving.

Fine wines are wonderful, but do get the temperature right. The reds should be 'chambré' and the whites chilled but not over-chilled. Make sure there is plenty of water. There is nothing more annoying than not having water . . . second thoughts probably worse not to have enough wine!

Leave the big things to the experts you have employed to do the job - the chefs, the waiters, the entertainers. Check the details in advance. The brown bread and butter - crusts on or off - the size of the lemon served with the fish dishes - so unnecessary to be mean with lemons - the quality of the coffee and how it is to be made. It is always the little things that let the side down.

Once you are happy with your concept for the evening, stick to it and plan every minute in detail. Decide on paper who is going to do what, live with it, re-write it if necessary and only then start briefing those who are helping. Give as much warning as you possibly can to whoever you wish to employ. Ring and have a chat with them to gain their commitment, and then meet with them to brief them about their role and where they fit into the overall scheme of the event. Confirm the basic details in writing, and make sure the job is costed and agreed. Agree the method of payment and when payment is to be made and stick to that as well. All this makes for a good working relationship, and then you can rely on them to do a great job. Just leave it to the experts, and enjoy yourself.

Arlette Bannister, Ackergill Tower

There is something magnificent about organising a weekend party for friends. With three or four food occasions as focal points you can create a marvellous range of informalities with more formal events. In order to have the most fun, the majority of the catering must simply be planned and cooked well in advance and, if it is at all possible, get some help. Most obviously the guests themselves will offer to help. Never turn this down, but equally don't rely on it. If you are properly organised, time in the kitchen ought to be minimal. You can probably judge the success of your weekend by how much time you have spent with your friends - planning as ever is crucial.

courtesy of Ackergill Tower

Planning the perfect weekend party

Planning is the secret to the perfect weekend party. Think of interesting things to do and see locally and plan meal times around your itinerary - remembering to be flexible.

Cold storage is vital when planning a large quantity of food in advance and it is well worth considering hiring an extra refrigerator for the weekend. Make sure the drinks cupboard is stocked up and remember the pre-lunch olives, nuts and crisps.

Saturday lunchtime could be a casual buffet style meal with a selection of cheeses, pâtés, quiches and salads served with crusty breads. If the weather is chilly then a bowl of good home-made soup always goes down well and this could be made on the Thursday and kept in the fridge until the Saturday lunchtime.

You may decide to give a dinner party for your guests on the Saturday evening. If so consider inviting some local friends who you think your guests would enjoy meeting and if you owe them hospitality you have killed two birds with one stone!

Here again the great thing is to make life easy and enjoyable for the hostess as well as the guests. The starter should be something that could be served with a simple garnish - for example a Stilton and mushroom mousse (prepared on the Friday and served in ramekin dishes) or egg mayonnaise with smoked salmon. The main course for a large number of guests must really be something that can be prepared a couple of days in advance, refrigerated and will re-heat perfectly, for example boeuf bourguinon, coq au vin or lamb with apricots. (One word of advice on preparing casseroles - always thicken with a roux and not cornflour otherwise the sauce will separate when re-heated and spoil the appearance.) Vegetables should be prepared in advance. Dauphinoise or Boulangère potatoes can be prepared and cooked the day before and will re-heat successfully making a more interesting addition to the meal. The sweet course could be something like oranges in Grand Marnier which could be prepared the day before and refrigerated. Avoid things that have to be decorated with whipped cream as these need to be completed on the day, but consider crème brulée or crème caramel which are always winners and can be prepared in advance. An ice-cream bombe would be a popular alternative.

Most people do not want any formality at breakfast time and it helps your guests feel relaxed and at home if you have available a good selection of cereals, fruit, toast, croissants, marmalade, jam and honey together with tea, coffee, chocolate and fruit juice to which they can help themselves. Eggs and bacon can be offered and cooked 'to order' as this does not take long and adds to the 'al fresco' feel of the meal. Remember to have plenty of extra milk as cereals take more than you think.

For Sunday lunch avoid the traditional roast if you want to spend maximum time with your guests and minimum time in the kitchen. Salmon fillets brushed with melted butter, sprinkled with lemon and parsley and wrapped in foil can be prepared on the Friday afternoon and refrigerated - put on a baking sheet and popped in the oven for approximately 30 minutes on the Sunday and are always very well received. Serve with new potatoes, baby carrots, baby sweetcorn, sugarsnap peas and hollandaise sauce - all of which can be purchased from good supermarkets if you are feeling too lazy to prepare them yourself! Pudding could be a warmed home-made apple pie taken from the freezer the previous evening and served with cream.

After all that, Sunday tea for your guests need only consist of a slice of home-made chocolate cake or fruit cake with a cup of tea and they will go merrily on their way feeling well fed and having enjoyed a relaxed and carefree weekend.

The success of the perfect weekend party must depend on planning good, easy to serve meals, buying and preparing everything before your guests arrive to enable you maximum time with them - after all that is the main reason for their visit! Consider whether any one has any special dietary needs, meticulously think through the menu and make lists of ingredients needed before you go shopping so as to avoid last minute panics!

Linda Baker, Linda's Pantry

Picnics, like all occasions, can either be simple or more lavish events. The two 'f's (arguably three) spring to mind - keeping food fresh and 'fings' not to forget - the following may hopefully inspire.

Picnics

September 2nd - Pangbourne on Thames

The journey up from Henley to Pangbourne, through Shiplake, Sonning and Reading was enjoyed by my entire crew, including our two dogs, Lottie and Elliot.

The venue for your picnic is of your choosing of course. Regarding the food and the surprise, I will share my ideas with you - appreciating that none of us has a monopoly on original ideas. We need to share them, for out of the sharing come enjoyment, friendship and fellowship (I trust any reader who agrees, disagrees or wishes to share ideas will write to me).

Picnics can be grand. They can take a lot of time, trouble and expense, but I feel to make them really memorable and enjoyable they should be practical, simple to prepare, light to carry and easy to eat.

What better place to consider the five Ps of picnics, than here at 'P' for Pangbourne listening to Vaughan Williams 'Lark Ascending' on the 'Sweet music' station!

The Five Ps of Picnics

- Plan
- Prep
- Pack
- Present
- Pleasure

Plan: If I asked you for a "de-brief" of your last three picnics I'm sure one of the major points you would record would be 'took too much'. Our aim is to travel light. It must be easy to pack and easy to carry.

From years of experience in assessing quantities for picnic hampers, I would suggest the following quantities per person:

Cooked Meats	200 grammes
Pâté	50 grammes
Smoked Fish	100 grammes
Smoked Salmon	50 grammes
Salads	Potato, Bavarian (see recipe in next section), Coleslaw, Assorted Bean 200 grammes
Lettuce	One standard tea cup
Tomato	One (or 3 cherry tomatoes)
Cucumber	One inch
Spring Onion	Two
Radish	Two
Bread Rolls	One white, one brown

Don't forget the long-standing favourite Ryvita (Light, Dark, Sesame). Allow one packet between four people and remember it is also ideal for cheese.

Forget French sticks, hard to pack and carry. Remember our aim is to travel light.

Dessert - only one per person, unless mini, then a maximum of three per person.

Fruit - not more than one and a half each. Fruit travels better if it is not chilled. Like red wine, room temperature is ideal. Don't ask what to do if weather is cold!

Write down a detailed list of what you are taking to eat and drink, what you need to pack it in, what you need to keep it cold/hot, what you need to eat it or drink it from and with, and other essentials to carefree picnicking like corkscrews, bottle openers, napkins, a bin liner, etc.

Prep: This is perhaps the most important part of the picnic - to ensure it is easy and enjoyable for all.

Usually, over 50% can be prepared one or two days before the picnic and this can be extended to weeks with the use of your freezer.

Just a little thought can make everything so much easier. I list a few suggestions, to which I am sure you will be able to add many more.

Extra small potatoes cooked in their skin while cooking the previous day's supper. They can be cut up quickly, mixed with the mayonnaise, chopped chives . . . all done and dusted within five minutes.

When roasting a whole chicken, remove and save the legs, thighs and wings (before serving the breast for your dinner). Coat the joints in your favourite coating, return them to the warm oven for 30 minutes and they are ready to be eaten cold the next day.

Then there are products which improve with time, and one of my favourites is Bavarian salad - (quantities for 4 people):

Red cabbage, finely sliced	250 grammes
Celery, sliced	100 grammes
Carrot, grated	100 grammes
Onion, sliced	100 grammes

All weights after trimming and cleaning. Mix together in a bowl, pour dressing over (recipe follows) and stir in lightly.

"Hot" Vinaigrette Sauce for Bavarian Salad:

5 fl oz vegetable oil
5 fl oz vinegar (cider or raspberry ideally)
1 level teaspoon ground mustard powder
Pinch of salt and a dusting of freshly ground black pepper.
Place all ingredients in a saucepan, bring to the boil, watching carefully. Remove from heat and allow to cool before adding to the prepared vegetables.

This salad needs at least a day to marinate, two days preferably, and should be stirred occasionally.

Should the picnic be a winter event, why not make your favourite styles of pasta in individual foil trays with cardboard lids? Heat prior to departure and place them in a thermal container which will keep them hot for several hours. Jacket potatoes can also be placed in such containers to be kept hot. Hot soup in a thermos is a Godsend at a chilly point-to-point.

Try to think of things that can be prepared the previous day, but take no health risks and do be sure that all prepared food is kept in a fridge.

With good 'prep' you will be able to control your kitchen clock which I find always seems to tick twice as fast as normal when the departure time for your picnic is approaching. Have you noticed this?

Pack: If you picnic regularly then I would recommend that you purchase a set of reusable plastic containers. On the other hand, every household has numerous non returnable containers which can be washed and made good. They are lightweight and ideal for packing your picnic food. Ice cream containers are a good example.

Traditional picnic baskets usually have specially designed containers and utensils. Remember to check the contents of the basket to make sure that no one "just borrowed" the corkscrew or the salt pot, and forgot to return them. Your imagination will be stretched trying to open a bottle of wine with a piece of wire or a rusty nail.

From your picnic plan (which I trust was written down!) check the items, crossing them off once packed. If you have company in the kitchen then occupy their time by asking them to do the checking. Speak out loud to avoid leaving anything behind. You haven't? I don't believe you!

One can place a great weight into the boot of a car, but if it has to be carried any distance at the other end (often the case at outdoor classical concerts) then pack into several easy-to-carry bags or baskets so everybody carries a fair weight.

Present: A picnic rug, a sheet of plastic and lightweight capes all help: comfort and 'insurance' against the elements.

Whilst a picnic is food 'in unusual surroundings', with these being the main attraction, don't overlook the culinary art of garnishing. A sprig of fresh parsley, the central stalks of celery with leaves, cherry tomatoes, not forgetting the wide range of attractive vegetables that can be used as a crudité with a light Madras dressing, these add a lot to the natural presentation of the picnic. Along with brightly coloured napkins and attractive disposable plates, use unbreakable plastic glasses for safety. There are some very good quality products available that can always be used at home on the patio or around the pool.

Every household has a vast supply of carrier bags - pack a couple of these for the picnic and then rubbish can be placed in them until you get home.

Pleasure: The final "P" to contemplate is pleasure in the drink.

Decisions about quantities are a personal matter, but bearing in mind the drink driving regulations I would allow no more than half a 75 cl bottle of wine per person or two cans of beer or lager per person, and I would include a selection of soft drinks for those who either don't drink or are driving.

Another reminder (my usual failing), don't forget the corkscrew and bottle opener. Alternatively, you can look out for screw cap wine bottles. I am sure, judging by the changing pattern from cork to artificial cork, there will be a many more wines with screw caps on the way in the near future, like our Lambrusco friends.

I trust some of my thoughts will inspire you to take meals to unusual places. Should you wish to enter into correspondence with me, I would welcome hearing your ideas, experiences and any unusual picnic problems solved on your feet. You can find my address at the back of this book under 'contributors'.

Should numbers or lack of time defeat your picnic plans then as the famous advert said "No I can't, but I know a man who does prepared picnics in quantity…"

Robert Spicer, Spicers of Hythe

As with so many parties the picnic is often affected by two items. Firstly, the location: it's up to you to try to out-think others - there is nothing worse than being surrounded. The second aspect is the weather - always have a wet weather plan!

courtesy of Stapleford Park

Sin & Tonic – for that wickedly good, ultimate party taste

Sin & Tonic from The London Gin Co. is the UK's first low alcohol gin & tonic premix. So now all those sociable, party-going people who really enjoy a good drink but also want to stay "in control", for whatever reason, can enjoy the refreshing flavour and appeal of a gin and tonic with almost none of the alcohol. An additional virtue of Sin & Tonic is that it contains fewer than 14 calories per 250 ml serving.

This means that it can be enjoyed for many different reasons, which should make it a "must have" for the ultimate party planner who is also the perfect host. Sin & Tonic's raison d'être is to fill a need in the low alcohol market for more palatable drinks. The product was developed by a leading industry expert who achieved an unprecedented quality of taste and resemblance to a normal gin and tonic. Party guests who are driving or counting calories or alcohol units or who simply would like a few glasses of wine after their aperitif but do not want a hangover the next day should all be willing to partake of a little Sin & Tonic

A further essential ingredient in the heady mix that is Sin & Tonic is its distinctive bottle with the memorable name which brings an immediate smile. The idea is that, even when not drinking alcohol, people at parties can have some fun by indulging in a "bit of Sin" - no longer the apologetic "no thanks", followed by an apology of a non-drink and a desperate search for something more interesting. Also if, as host or hostess, you wish to keep a clear head whilst welcoming guests, but without putting a dampener on proceedings, you might wish to indulge in some secret Sin!

Sin & Tonic, London Gin Co.

courtesy of The Ice Box

THE ʟᴏᴡ ALCOHOL
GIN FIZZER

from THE LONDON GIN COMPANY Ltd.

That special touch

That special touch

That special touch

That special touch

That special touch

That special touch

That special touch

That special touch

That special touch

That special touch

That special touch

That special touch

So you've finally thought of a good theme for your shindig and this seems like a great idea in the morning and you can afford it and you have got the time to plan it and you ... What are those little extras you might need to take into consideration to make the event as original and as organised as possible?

To some fancy dress is anathema, others love dressing up but not always in public, others just can't wait to reveal themselves in a ridiculous costume. When planning parties it is best to try to consider the majority of your guests. Your best pal Maurice might have a rubber fetish but that does not mean everybody has a ready made suit. Successful themes are often those that allow a variety of dress - black and white is the most obvious but does it necessarily rule out the Newcastle United strip? Consider how the theme can be applied to your invitations, your catering and decoration but most of all avoid putting people off. There are all manner of themes you can adopt but the most successful is usually the most simple.

The Party Superstore

Peeks have been supplying decorations to match food and drink themes (like Valentine's Day, Caribbean, etc) for 20 years. They now offer over one hundred themes in their catalogue and items are available either individually or in theme packs. The catalogue is available to anyone from a private partygiver to a large event organiser. Having studied the party business in the United States over the past 10 years, Peeks have now launched a new venture - the Party Superstore.

THEMES

In addition to the usual themes such as Independence Day, Beaujolais Nouveau, Patron Saints' Days and National Days, there are a number of more obscure themes for organisers to consider:

- Burns' Night - January 25th
- Battle of the Alamo - February 23rd
- Buffalo Bill's Birthday - February 26th - for a Wild West Night
- St. Trinian's Day - March 23rd - great for school days and so easy for dressing up!
- Australia Discovered - April 28th - hang Christmas decorations upside down!
- Buddy Holly's Birthday - September 7th - Rock 'n' Roll!
- Blackbeard died - November 22nd 1718 - Pirate theme

THEME DECORATING - SOME HELPFUL HINTS

- Don't try to decorate the entire function room unless you have a large budget. Concentrate instead on focal points - food serving areas, for example.
- Props are not always easy to obtain, and their availability may affect the theme you decide to adopt.
- Order your theme packs or the individual items well in advance.
- Penny saving idea: keep the decorations in the box, and use them to complement a future theme event. For example, items from our tropical range can be used again for a pirate theme party in future.
- If you want balloon decorating, you can use some of our items to create a 3-D effect. The 6ft jointed palm tree with tissue parrots used with yellow and green balloons can be most effective.

COLOUR THEME DECORATING

Balloons are the cheapest way to achieve a colour theme. A simple way to produce a bunch of 4-colour coordinating balloons is to knot each balloon, tie two pairs of balloons together by the neck, then wrap the balloons around each other to create your bunch. Use coordinating curled ribbon tape to complete the effect. Alternatively, get professional balloon decorators to create balloon arches and balloon sculptures using your proposed colour scheme.

Table decorating can be quite simple. If your caterer cannot supply different coloured tablecloths use white and then co-ordinate the colours of the napkins to your colour theme.

MENUS

All caterers have access to specialist catering companies who can offer food to match all the most popular themes. You can have some fun with the menu though, as can be seen from the following:

NAUTICAL MENU

Neptune's Nuggets (Cod Fishcakes)
Portholes (Battered Calamari Rings)
Star Fish (Breaded Sea Stars)
Pirate's Paella
Captain Hook's Cocktail (Prawn Cocktail)
Shiver Me Timbers (Crispy Prawn Brochettes)
Not Jaws! (Crispy Cod Bites)
Sea Chest (Seafood Baskets)
Mizzen Masts (Oriental King Prawn Rolls)
Shoals of Fish (Whitebait)
Lobster Pot (Lobster Meat)

FANCY DRESS

In America most parties seem to involve some form of fancy dress but it will take some time before we reserved Brits overcome our reluctance to dress up for parties. Dressing up can also involve a lot of time and effort if you have to make the costumes. Most people are prepared to accept some form of simple accessory, such as Hawaiian leis for tropical theme events, and these are readily available.

A huge range of fancy dress costumes imported from the United States is available from the Party Superstore. They are one size and available on a purchase collection basis. This saves time and trouble on making costumes, and is no more expensive than costume hire.

OTHER PARTY IDEAS TO CONSIDER

Murder Mystery - plenty of choice of themed decoration kits which can be purchased with Murder Mystery Packs, very easy to run and great fun.

Casino Nights - simple to organise and conforming to the Lotteries Act as only fun money is used. Prizes are usually offered to those with the most money at the end of the event.

Quiz Nights - most companies offer quiz packs with questions based on a choice of themes.

Race Nights - very exciting events which can be used by fund raisers or fun raisers.

Fireworks - most companies have a large range of fireworks that can be fired by the non-professional, with full safety and firing instructions supplied.

Millennium Celebrations - the mind boggles, the possibilities are endless, and it is not too soon to start planning now!

*Robert Eveleigh,
Peeks the Event
Makers*

courtesy of Banana Split

If theming a party might cause concern then an entertainer is an excellent way of providing your guests with something unusual and memorable without the problems associated with dressing up. There are all manner of performers today from music to mime and from juggling to jesting… But do try to pick the right entertainer for your special occasion. I recall the most marvellous birthday party for which an "operagramme" had been organised. The trouble was she arrived when most of the party were more than a little merry and the resultant "let's sing along boys because we know the words" somewhat marred the effect.

Getting the best from your budget

The cost of organising live entertainment has never been more varied and although the professional organiser should be aware of these extremes, the new organiser has few opportunities to make direct comparisons.

In the sixties and seventies, large scale events were invariably held in hotels or conference halls and entertainment programmes were usually considered only when all the food and beverage requirements had been negotiated. The entertainment had to be planned from the remains of the budget. In a few cases there was a separate budget but almost invariably the story was "fish course *or* the speciality dinner music!"

Events have moved to unusual locations, guests eat less and certainly drink less both for reasons of diet and out of social responsibility. There are still notable exceptions, seasonal goodwill at Christmas being one, but by and large the total emphasis on food and beverage as the major ingredients has been eclipsed.

There are now extra ingredients of which entertainment is just one. The others are presentation and scene setting - ambience achieved through staging, lighting, sound, decor and special effects. Success means paying attention to these ingredients and the emphasis has to depend on the location and the occasion.

Most importantly, it is a question of getting a balance between the ingredients and the best value from your budget. This is why we recommend seeking professional advice on the cost of different entertainment options.

Some of the most successful events that we have arranged have not been those with a huge entertainment budget. Simple ideas that are modest in cost can, in some circumstances, be as effective as bespoke productions. The rule is to list your objectives, taking into account some key questions.

- Will the guests be present or do they need to be attracted to the event?
- What is the span of the event?
- What do the location and facilities call for?
- What is the mix and age group of the guests?
- What style of food service is envisaged?
- What message do we wish to convey?
- What precedents have been set and how can we improve on previous events?

At this stage it is useful to try to set a budget, remembering that your figures need to be split between fixed and variable costs. From an entertainment point of view, most expensive does not necessarily mean most suitable for the occasion. Speakers and presenters for business and social events start at around £500 but rise to £20,000 and more. Do you actually need a top TV celebrity? Bands start at the same modest figure and rise to around £3000. Discotheques start at £250 and rise to £1500. If you are prepared to pay the higher levels you need to know what you are getting for your money! Invariably the figures are based on supply and demand and, of course, reputation.

A word on negotiation. While there should always be an element of flexibility on pricing, the budget first quoted should be fair and realistic. If the buying remit covers a number of dates, the purchasing power is increased. Day of the week, time of the day, season of the year all contribute to the pricing structure and a good adviser will take advantage of these factors on your behalf.

Huge budgets can buy results but more modest budget allocations demand close attention to achieve the desired results. See that you get the attention your event deserves.

Peter Richardson, Fanfare 3000

So what was the greatest party ever? Well, there have been a few - I guess the end of the World Wars must have been something else - demonstrating that atmosphere and occasion are rivals for good food and drink, both of which were in limited supply back then. Naturally, the year 2000 millennium party will also test the partygoer and organiser. There are all manner of little extras to consider. Some may have been around years ago, others are more recent developments, all are great fun.

A spectacular firework display

You've organised the very best caterers at the most stunning venue, and now you are looking for that extra sparkle to complete the evening's entertainment.

Fireworks are still something of a novelty at private parties or weddings and may just provide the perfect ending - or highlight - to the day. A spectacular burst of noise and colour never fails to dazzle and delight the audience, be they 9 or 90 years of age. Keeping the whole thing a secret until the first ker-boom! can really top off the day, especially for a surprise 40th or for sending the bride and groom off with a bang.

Fireworks aren't just the preserve of chilly November nights huddled around a bonfire but can be a year-round phenomenon. Summer concerts with fireworks are proving a popular combination and setting your display to music could well be another party option - round off the evening with a blast from the 1812, or a rousing piece of Pomp for a truly memorable occasion.

A special set-piece could also make your show unique with the name of a loved one, a personal message or company logo lit up in fireworks and glitter.

So, where and how do you start organising a firework display? You'll have too much on your plate to even think about doing it yourself, and, like the catering or the flower arrangements, it is something that is best left to professionals.

courtesy of Searcy's & Joanna Plumbe Photography

A large area isn't always necessary for the actual firing zone. It is the 'fall out' area that is more crucial. A site safety survey will determine whether or not there is sufficient space away from buildings, parked cars and the audience. The show will be designed accordingly to suit both your requirements and those of the venue itself.

You will be sent a detailed, costed proposal which will include the site safety survey, the design, setting up and firing of the show by fully trained operators, as well as the necessary insurance cover.

So, what are you waiting for? Whatever the time of year, whatever the weather and whatever the occasion, fireworks must be top of the list for your perfect party.

Indoor table fountains

You don't need a garden the size of a football pitch or even access to an outdoor terrace to enjoy pyrotechnical delights at your special party.

A brand-new, unique product now available for the fun party market is the indoor 'Table Fountain'. Specially designed to be debris and smoke-free, these will add some major sparkle to your do. You can almost hear Q saying to 007 "Now here's a cunning little device, James"!

Arranged and well-hidden amongst floral centrepieces, the gold or silver cascading fountains are detonated by remote control with no tell-tale wires or fuses in sight. Fantastic for Christmas parties and perfect for creating a stir during the after-dinner speeches, the Table Fountains can be kept a secret until the moment they explode.

Up to forty tables can be primed in this way, so whether your party is a small gathering or a swell affair these safe but exciting giant sparklers will be certain to add glitter to the occasion!

Samantha Whitton, Pains Fireworks Ltd

courtesy of Pains Fireworks

Special touches

There are almost unlimited possibilities you can choose from to make your party really special and different, and here are just a few examples. Using all of these ideas would be possible theoretically if your pocket were deep enough, but most people would probably cherry-pick the ones they particularly liked or that fitted in best with the occasion and the theme of the event.

FACE PAINTING

"Oh, do you do parties?" parents say, when they hear I am a member of FACE The Face Painting Association.

Little do they know just how incredibly popular face painting and body painting have become in the serious party-giving world. It is not just for kids any more, although they are still our number one clients. One of the reasons that body painting is a must at adult parties is that the guests have missed out on a craze which children have been enjoying since the mid '80s. The widespread availability of easily removable water-based make-up has brought back into fashion the '60s fascination with body decoration. This time it's back with a vengeance and it is not just for the mean and moody.

Body painting is a huge ice breaker as inevitably people gather round to admire or perhaps laugh at the latest model's new look. This can range from applying paint to part of the body to the 'Full Monty', which can bring a touch of the truly exotic to a party. Imagine walking past an alcove and glancing at a statue only to find it winks back at you, or finding that the Egyptian slave statues standing on either side of the entrance to a marquee are real flesh and blood. It is sometimes hard to believe that these statues are real people when they are painted with weathered cracks and verdigris. The temptation to touch, just to be sure, is compelling. Perhaps made up to look like a bronze, 'Living Statues' are devastatingly realistic and an endless fascination.

Full body painting comes into its own where there is a requirement to shock without causing offence. Topless waitresses with painted-on basques feel quite modest and comfortable in their painted clothes. Guests who want to stare can, as in Victorian times, claim to be admiring the art rather than the nude. The only problem with creating this sort of impact is finding somewhere warm for your painted models to wait in comfort. A painted fur coat is not as cosy as the real thing and dancers' muscles have to be looked after. Not long ago I painted two beautiful dancers as a tiger and a blue cat so that they could appear after dinner dancing to jungle music. More recently I have painted a young man in bold Maori warpaint style. He was performing a traditional Maori dance at a reception at London Zoo. Getting dancers to perform in minimal clothes may be a new trend and as someone who has been privileged to paint many beautiful bodies I can see the attraction.

As an entertainment, body painting is surprisingly convenient as it does not take up a lot of space. All you need are two chairs and a small table usually provided by the artist. Of course the artist needs to be situated where there is good light. If there are staff or members of the family to be made up, the artist should be booked to arrive in time to start work about an hour before the party. A full body make-up takes approximately one to one and a half hours for each model and does require a warm room with some privacy, though some artists and models are prepared to

courtesy of Searcy's & Joanna Plumbe Photography

work in public as part of the entertainment. Artists and models should be consulted about timing and length of performance in advance as there are so many variables depending on the design and the height of the models. The smaller body decorations take only three to five minutes each which makes them ideal as people don't have to wait a long time.

Whatever sort of entertainment you are arranging, plan well ahead. Ask for written confirmation that the booking has been accepted and be prepared to sign a contract or at least give written confirmation of the venue address, date, time, the fee and what is required of the artiste. This is always expected by a professional artiste and protects you as well as them. It is too late to complain after the party if the entertainment was disappointing so book people who have been recommended or those whose work you have seen. Better still, go through an organisation such as The Face Painting Association or an entertainment agency.

Caro Childs, FACE The Face Painting Association

SIMULATION

The Venture Simulator is based on the sophisticated technology developed for the multi-million pound flight-simulators used to train astronauts, jet fighter pilots and airline pilots. Simulation combines the powerful effect of motion with an eye-view film to create a new form of entertainment which is enjoyable, exciting, stimulating and completely safe.

In the simulator you can experience - in sight, sound and motion - such thrills as flying a Harrier Jump Jet, coming down the Olympic bBobsleigh run at 90 mph, or the sensation of being a crash-test dummy zooming round the test centre. It is not for the faint-hearted!

After only a few seconds of simulated experience the human instincts of survival and self-preservation take over. You stop thinking 'this is only a moving capsule and some pictures'. Your mind perceives as real what it is experiencing and starts thinking about surviving the 90 mph descent.

The simulator combines experience, education and thrills and can offer much more than just entertainment. It can be an extremely effective marketing tool by being themed to reflect a corporate style, a brand image or a special concept. With high profile graphics and theming, a simulator can create unique visibility, awareness and media cover for corporate identity or PR campaigns.

What better way to make your private party or function unique and memorable?

Sue Tuck, S & D Leisure Simulation Services

ICE SCULPTURES

The introduction of an ice sculpture to an event or party is a unique and novel way to create a centrepiece and support a theme.

The variety of ways in which ice can be used is almost endless. On a simple level, a giant clam shell can be carved and used for displaying seafood. At the other end of the spectrum are fantastic skilfully carved sculptures with channels skilfully carved to shoot vodka through. "Ice Luges", as these are called, take their name from the famous Cresta Run in St. Moritz. They are now a 'must have' at really happening parties, especially for after dinner entertainment.

Ice sculptures are also very popular at corporate functions to display company logos and even products. A multitude of items from beauty products to canned and bottled drinks, even record-players and computers, have been frozen inside ice which is then crafted as a sculpture.

And then there is the ultimate ice sculpture: a complete bar made

courtesy of The Ice Box

71

from ice. The whole bar is constructed of large decorated blocks of ice and is used by the bar staff to serve the guests. Ideal as a vodka bar - the bar counter can be adapted to hold bottles of vodka inside wells to keep it frozen.

Don't worry about it melting too fast. An ice bar will last for days if left alone in a cool place. Avoiding direct sunlight and draughts will help too.

Philip Hughes, The Ice Box

WATER SCULPTURES

Water can be used in a vast range of ways from a wedding cake rising majestically from the centre of a fountain to a wall of coloured water cascading down the sides of your marquee (without getting anything wet!). It is possible to create fountains inside stately homes, to incorporate floral displays into a 16 foot wide waterfall, and strew colourful bubble tubes between pillars to create a magical atmosphere in a half light situation.

Just about the only thing that is impossible to do is get water to run uphill!

Byll Elliot, Water Sculptures Ltd

ENTERTAINMENT EQUIPMENT

After booking the room, deciding on the food, arranging for a disco or band you are still looking for something to make the evening really memorable. Fun entertainment equipment is what you need. Trying to stay on the Surf Simulator at the beach party evening, or riding the Bucking Bronco at the Wild West evening will prove to be really memorable for you and your guests.

The three suggestions given below are a small part of the range of equipment available, and the range is expanding almost daily.

Giant Scalextric Racing: You can choose from the Brands Hatch or Silverstone four track circuit giving you the thrills and spills of Formula One racing using miniature replicas of the real thing.

Bungee Running: Strap yourself into the harness which is attached to the bungee cord. Make sure you have your velcro marker firmly in your grip, ready to place down on the marked and measured strip between the two lanes. Then run as hard and as fast and as far down your lane as you can and mark your final resting place!

Gyroscope: Could this be a spin-off from NASA? Surely astronauts can't have this much fun? You don't even need to be level-headed to enjoy hours of safe fun spinning on two different axes.

Keith Mitchell, 1st Leisure Supplies

BALLOONS

No party is complete without balloons. The range of products available to the party organiser today is almost limitless.

courtesy of Searcy's & Joanna Plumbe Photography

Latex balloons are available from 5 inches to 10 feet, and are available in a range of colours to match any theme. Specialist shops now stock a vast range of latex balloons in designer colours and many of them have standard stock printed balloons ready made for your event.

Foil or metallic balloons come in all shapes and sizes and there are even ones that will walk around the room.

Specialist venue decorators can create amazing effects with balloons - tunnels, arches, bowers, waterfalls, sculptures, canopies. The sky is the limit - especially in the case of balloon releases.

NABAS

Many people like to overcomplicate, others cannot delegate - both tendencies provide recipes for disaster. As Thoreau said: "Our life is frittered away by detail... simplify, simplify".

Under Cover

There's something special about marquees. You don't tend to see them at sombre affairs, you rarely see them in winter and when you're in one you're usually at a party or occasion of interest . . . a sporting event perhaps, or a fair. Yes, marquees are pretty likeable fellows.

Or are they . . . ? While they may signify good times, their erection is usually the culmination of considerable effort in thought and word and deed. Furthermore, the mere fact that something large and white is appearing in your garden is indicative that much work probably remains to be done. The flame has been lit, but much can be done and must be done to ensure the beacon shines brightly for all to admire.

What to avoid

Imagine the scene - it's your precious daughter's wedding day and you've hired a marquee for the reception. You haven't had time to check, but you trust that tables and chairs have been set out, the bar and buffet look deliciously tempting and the finishing touches have been made to floral displays. Nothing could possibly go wrong . . .

But as Murphy's Law would have it, things do!

There are horror stories of tables and chairs being handed to guests as they arrived, four-tier wedding cakes collapsing from the heat in the marquee and crossed electrical wires in the mobile toilets giving guests electric shocks when they pulled the chain after spending a penny!

So how could you avoid disaster? If you decide to hire a marquee, contractors should provide you with the tent itself, suitable flooring such as timber or carpeting and a lining - whether plain, ruched or pleated. They should also supply furniture to suit the occasion whether gilt banqueting chairs or white plastic seats, tables up to six feet in diameter, trestle tables for the buffet and a bar and bar tables. Other essentials are lighting, heating and toilets.

MUTA (Made-Up Textiles Association) have put together the following tips:

- Choose a MUTA member to supply and erect your marquee. MUTA is the recognised trade association policing safety standards for marquees. Members must meet specified criteria to be certified and spot checks are regularly carried out to ensure that they are using flame-retardant materials and that tents are erected to the standards set in our Code of Practice.

- Every host has a responsibility for the safety of his or her guests. If you choose a MUTA member you can be sure the contractor complies with our standards. If something does go wrong you have the reassurance that MUTA will put pressure on a member to settle any dispute in an amicable and reasonable way.

- Get quotes from a number of contractors - and don't always plump for the cheapest option.

Hiring a marquee can cost anything from £800 to £40,000 depending on your requirements so quotes also vary—like everything else, you get what you pay for. If you can, it's a good idea to inspect a marquee that your chosen contractor has already erected so that you know what to expect. Very often the only difference between contractors is in the final appearance - so it's a good idea to look before you choose.

- Think carefully about the theme and setting you want. You should discuss your needs in detail with your contractor, so that you

75

are not disappointed with the final result. Consider the effect you want to achieve. If the setting is traditional, you may want to choose a canvas marquee, while if it is modern, you may want to plump for a PVC covered aluminium-framed marquee.

- Think, too, about the interior. A lining should always be provided, because however new a marquee is, it will have blemishes that would otherwise show through. Finally, consider whether you need windows and what type of emergency exits to include.

- Be mindful of the season of the year and choose the best option to withstand possible bad weather. Selecting a marquee to suit the time of year is essential. Generally, if you are worried about weather conditions, a frame-supported marquee is the best all-year-round choice. If snow is a 53possibility, then heating equipment should be fitted with a frost stat to melt ice before it forms. Marquees are not designed to with stand huge falls of snow and will collapse.

courtesy of The Marquee Company

- Make sure the marquee is well anchored to the ground by the contractors. It may seem obvious, but if ground anchors are not properly fitted, the marquee is at risk of collapsing or taking off. Don't remove any fitting without asking first or you could destabilise the marquee.

- If the marquee material looks more than five years old, ask if it has been tested to make sure it is still flame retardant. If the marquee needs to be erected by a certain date and time, have that written into the hire contract. You could otherwise be disappointed - but you must also bear in mind that it could add to the final cost.

Perhaps I should have got the marquee
from a MUTA approved supplier!

Mike Bunting, MUTA Made-Up Textiles Association

You can either do it or you can't - it's either in you or not - and you know what I'm talking about - of course you do - putting up a tent. Let's face it some of us are practical and others, like me, are not. Today, so many 'Ikeaesque' items are self-assembly… it's enough to drive a man to drink - which is frankly the only good that can be said of it. Putting up a marquee always looks simple, but as with everything, simplicity and quality are found in the hands of the experts and not every firm can be given such praise.

I recently had the pleasure of attending a corking wedding. The sun shone, the bride cried at the altar (but still got married!). All was well with the world. What's more it didn't stop there. The reception was in a delightful country house, used for weddings, conferences and that sort of thing, and did everyone proud. A marquee had been attached, for the summer I gather, at the end of a walled garden - it was fairly simple in design but the walled garden added so much character to the affair. Perhaps what impressed me most was the food - not Le Manoir aux Quat' Saisons - but delicious and everything served at the right temperature. So it can be done, but in my view, to get this critical ingredient of the day right, near military planning is required and it is your caterer who is surely your foremost general.

Staging an event in a marquee

So, you've decided to hold the Party of the Year. The only problem is that your house is too small (or you have too many good friends!). You are left with a number of alternatives.

- Hold the party in a hotel. This can be much more costly, the food can be a little institutional or dull, the drinks are very expensive and the whole affair can seem a bit - well - antiseptic and unimaginative, unless you are prepared to throw a lot of money at it.

- Hold the party in a venue which specialises in big do's. You may be able to bring in your own caterer, but often you are tied to using one from a preferred list. If you do bring in your own caterers you may be subject to surcharges. The venue may wish to supply the drink (after all, they are in business to make money!), or charge hefty corkage if you insist on bringing in the special reserve that you have been saving for just such an occasion. And, depending on zoning restrictions, unless the venue has a late licence, they may have to stop serving drinks at midnight or even 11.00 pm, and music may have to stop by then as well.

But wait! What about your own rose garden/the field next door/the tennis court? How about a marquee? There is a certain feeling of grandeur and romance about staging a party in a marquee. Certainly there are advantages to being able to…

- house/seat a greater number of people. This is particularly useful if you are hosting a fund-raising event - more people, more money - as hotels and other fixed venues will have space limitations
- provide shelter against the elements
- have exactly the sort of food you want and the freedom to produce all the booze which you quietly amassed on your last trip to France
- decorate/theme the area exactly the way you want it.

As caterers, we have all sorts of experience working in marquees . . the following pointers should really be entitled 'Words from the Wise', or 'Things you may not have considered (which the marquee company won't necessarily tell you)'.

For the purposes of this example, let's assume that this party is going to start with a reception, followed by a sit-down meal and then dancing.

SIZE MATTERS

Well, it does. A lot. Marquee companies tend to forget about the needs of the poor caterer. If you tell them you are having a sit-down dinner for 150, they will tell you that you need a tent measuring 50 ft by 30 ft. End of story. This doesn't necessarily take into account any space for the reception, the bar, the dance floor. Some tables can of course be removed to reveal a fabulous dance floor reminiscent of Saturday Night Fever - but where are all the newly table-less to sit when they are not dancing?

As caterers, we often find ourselves presented with a 'fait accompli' where marquees are concerned. Of course we recognise budget constraints, but we would strongly recommend that you speak to your caterer before finalising the size of the marquee. Caterers can often point out limitations and pitfalls which marquee companies don't care about. The marquee company's job is to put the thing up. If these potential pitfalls are pointed out in advance, they can usually be resolved but they can cause major dramas if discovered an hour prior to the arrival of the guests.

MARQUEE COWBOYS

Whilst there are many very good and highly reputable marquee companies around, there are also a number of cowboys. These are easily recognised by not having an office with a phone (or at least they are never there when you call), by only being contactable via their mobiles, and by being difficult to pin down about exactly the sort of tent they are selling you ("Yeah, this tent'll fit that number of guests, no problem"). Start to worry if they will not provide you with a scale drawing showing precise measurements, positioning of windows, supports/guy wires, doorways (these can have considerable impact on the positioning of tables), are more than vague about lighting, tables and chairs (if they are providing them), and are reluctant to show you any photographs of their marquees in action. Often these companies won't even submit a written quotation, preferring a Gentleman's Agreement, sealed with a handshake and with prices and dimensions written on the back of an envelope (yes, dear readers, I have seen this!). Granted, these companies are less expensive, and are undoubtedly adept at making a great sales pitch, but at the end of the day you have to decide whether you need the additional stress of wondering whether the company will turn up to erect the tent, whether it will be sturdy enough to withstand the rigours of the British weather (I have heard of ones which have collapsed at the 11th hour because of high winds), and whether you have sufficient Rescue Remedy to see you through the ordeal!

TIME SCHEDULES

In our experience, marquees never quite manage to be finished on schedule. Sometimes the problems are unavoidable. We once catered for a party of 500 and torrential non-stop rain for the three days prior to the event left us with no option but to call in the Fire Service to pump out a foot of water from inside the marquee. Chefs and kitchen staff were attractively attired in Wellington boots on that occasion! Other times the problems can be due to inadequate planning. Our advice is if you can possibly afford to have the tent erected two or three days prior to the party it will save you no end of hassle.

SERVICE TENT

No matter what type of catering you are planning, it is essential to provide a service tent on the back of the marquee - or if not attached, then linked with a covered walkway. This area does not require lining or flooring although from a safety point of view flooring is preferable. It will obviously require power points and must be a minimum of 20 ft by 20 ft to allow sufficient space for cooking as well as for cleaning. This service area is often forgotten about by marquee companies and clients alike, but is essential. If in doubt about the size, speak to your caterer who will provide you with their requirements based on the menu you have chosen.

POWER

Power is essential if you plan on having a band, lighting, hot food, twinkly lights on the ceiling . . . sadly these items cannot be run from your house mains unless your house is normally lit up like the Blackpool Illuminations. It is advisable to use a lighting or power company who are used to working with marquees, and who can ensure that you have plenty of power to run all of the equipment at the same time. If a kitchen is using electric ovens, hot cupboards, hot water urns, etc, it is likely that all this equipment will be used simultaneously.

Recently, we catered for a wedding in a field adjacent to a farm. Despite many veiled and not so veiled warnings from us to hire a reputable spark, we were assured that the farm circuits would be able to cope. Wrong. As soon as the portable loos started being used all the kitchen power was lost. Once the guests had sat down for their first course, the Best Man got up and asked everyone who had to go to the loo to go then so that the loos could be turned off and we could cook the main course! So much for spontaneity.

As far as the service tent is concerned, your caterer will have a pretty clear idea of exactly where power points are required. The marquee company's idea of a plug hanging down from the middle of the ceiling with 16 extension leads trailing from it may be neither safe nor efficient. Let's face it, it makes sense to ask the people who are going to be spending the better part of a day/evening in there. After all, if marquee companies were experts in the culinary arts they wouldn't be in the marquee business. And when organising lights, please don't forget the poor chefs - it is terribly difficult to create spun sugar nests by candlelight.

WATER

A water point in close proximity is useful and a hose will do if there is no tap nearby. Urns and chafing dishes will need filling, and there is always the odd bit of washing up (too many glasses of champagne being quaffed may require a bit of rapid washing, drying and polishing).

FURNITURE

Most marquee companies prefer to provide you with the tables and chairs. If you can, get them to bring in a sample chair and table just to make certain the equipment is in good nick, and that the chairs are comfortable, the right colour, etc. Many marquee companies hire in the equipment (only the really large companies keep stocks in-house), in which case it is worth checking with your caterer who may be willing to give you a package deal for all equipment.

LOOS

Depending on where your marquee is located, loos may need to be brought in. These are useful if you don't particularly want 150 people trekking through your house in search of the facilities. These days portable loo units are positively swanky, and even the most basic can be tarted up with some decent loo paper, a few hand towels and a pretty flower arrangement.

CATERING

The most important part of the evening. Really! Guests will always remember two things: the food and the service. If either is lacking it will be remarked upon and remembered, thereby demoting your party to 'just missed being the event of the season'.

If money is no object, and providing there is sufficient space for cooking and preparation, there are really no limits to what a caterer can produce in a site kitchen. Caterers will ask you all sorts of questions about how you envisage the evening unfolding, what arrangements you have made regarding the marquee, service tent, power, etc, and will then be able to come up with no end of suggestions to suit the facilities available. Unless you really do have loads of space, loads of staff, and an unlimited budget, I strongly advise you to keep the menu simple. Simple dishes, beautifully cooked, using the freshest ingredients available and presented attractively are hard to beat.

BRINGING ALL THE ELEMENTS TOGETHER

If you are using different suppliers for equipment, food, lighting, flowers, music, etc, timing needs to be co-ordinated carefully so that the florist doesn't arrive to install huge floral centrepieces before the roof and lighting have been finished and all the tables have been placed and laid up.

Best advice - treat the whole event as a finely tuned military operation. Careful planning and scheduling are essential and will save you endless worry, time and money later on.

Once the candles are lit, the guests have arrived and the first glass of champagne is poured, you will forget all about the little hiccups and be ready to enjoy a spectacular evening.

Amanda Stephenson, Gorgeous Gourmets

courtesy of Searcy's & Joanna Plumbe Photography

Organising a marquee and the numerous trappings that can go with them is something that has to be planned and orchestrated smoothly. Last minute changes must be avoided if at all possible. Furthermore, try to find a well-established firm. There are some horrific tales of woe and choosing a MUTA member has to be a sensible idea. From the humble wedding to events as diverse as the Grand Prix and the Chelsea Flower Show, these chaps are there and what they don't know about a good erection isn't worth knowing!

So without further ado, as people tend to say somewhat tiresomely at weddings, over to . . . the Marquee Company

Marquee hire guide

SOME DOS AND DON'TS

Do: Make initial enquiries as soon as is practically possible - the best firms are usually booked earliest.

Don't: Rely on the great British weather. I'd like a pound for every wet Friday that brought a phone enquiry for 150 guests the next day.

Do: Insist on a site meeting (good suppliers will insist themselves!) to avoid last minute hitches.

Don't: Overlook guest parking - is there sufficient space nearby? When guests leave is there sufficient temporary lighting back to cars?

Do: Remember to arrange suitable facilities for disabled or infirm guests.

Don't: Crowd your guests, allow approximately 1.5 m^2 or 15 ft^2 per guest for dining plus dancing, reception and bar areas.

Do: Plan layouts with your supplier carefully—for example, bars should be well away from dance floors. Plan space for bad weather contingencies and allow room for buffets and/or service access. A good supplier will provide tailor-made plans as a matter of course.

Don't: Forget to discuss arrangements for heavy vehicles. Although professional suppliers will not damage lawns under any circumstances, it's as well to be clear about what's permitted.

courtesy of Searcy's & Joanna Plumbe Photography

Do: Cut lawns 2 days before the agreed installation date.

Don't: Take short cuts with heating arrangements. A good marquee company will only allow the use of ducted hot air heaters with thermostat controls and no naked flames. Space heaters should not even be considered.

Do: Ensure suitable flooring is installed. The options are: matting or woven floor covering - inexpensive but prone to tripping points if not laid properly; carpeting; or, best of all (if budgets allow), a wooden interlocking sub floor with carpet, which is a must on hard surfaces such as Tarmac or concrete so that water can run under the floor.

Don't: Take risks with electrics. Involve a qualified elec-trician and if in any doubt have him on standby for the event. If nearby power is not available there are some very efficient and super silent modern generators available via your marquee contractor.

Do: Check that all is as you expected before your installation crew depart. It is part of our company's procedure to "walk the course" with every client before final departure.

Don't: Employ any marquee company that does not comply to the relevant BS standards or cannot produce a MUTA safety certificate.

Do: Look after your installation crew! You'll be surprised what good effect the odd cuppa or cooling drink will have!

AND FINALLY . . .

Do: Sit back and enjoy the celebrations, secure in the knowledge that all is under control. Remember - in hotel settings, the hotel gets the compliments, but in a marquee at home it's all yours! Enjoy the party and take all of the credit for weeks to come!

Stephen Keyes, The Marquee Company

courtesy of The Marquee Company

Flowers can add a lot to any occasion. They imply growth and vitality, they suggest freshness and life, they offer colour and fragrance. They also die. Looking after flowers, as with all aspects of your party, requires imagination and good timing.

When people organise a wedding, plants are often used twice: in the church and at the reception. I remember once coming a cropper on the church steps transforming a beautiful floral display into a squashed mess with great effect and a good deal of pain!

Flowers in a marquee

THE PLANNING STAGES

- Make time to visit the site, check access and ensure you allow enough time to cover the unexpected.
- Always check with the caterers regarding access times, space, etc, to ensure that both of you are aware of all arrangements, have the same information and have compatible ideas on settings and accessories.
- Talk to the marquee hire company and check the positions of dance floor, heaters, fire exits, poles and rigging, and - most important - lighting.
- Ensure that you are included in any site visits that might result in last minute changes.
- Always provide sketches and examples of your ideas beforehand.
- Keep your ideas simple.
- Try and provide a "show stopper" at the entrance.
- Allow for weather.
- When deciding on a colour scheme, take into account the lighting and the time of day.
- Space is usually at a premium in a marquee, so remember that flowers, garlands and floral features always look stunning if suspended well above people's heads alongside lighting.
- When choosing your flowers, take into account the season, what foliage is available and select only the best quality so that you can condition and prepare them beforehand.
- Try to include both interior and exterior displays. Entering through gardens, a floral arch or some sort of extravaganza can put the guests into the party mood.
- If working to a theme, ensure that any props are away from the busy areas and are neither too fragile nor too easily moved.
- Try to incorporate some seasonal flowers and foliage into your displays.

Russell, Twining & Bere Ltd

courtesy of The Marquee Company

While the food you choose may be complex, the booze you choose can be simple. If you agree with that you'll go along with anything! Variety is the spice of life and exciting drinks can be prepared with some ease but remember don't provide too much and don't thrust it down people. Don't leave them dry, but don't soak them before the main event gets under way.

Today the choice of wines, beers, cocktails, champagnes and after-dinner drinks is extraordinary but as ever help is at hand, in the form of your your local wine merchant. In this day and age there are all manner of incentives - not least free wine tasting and free glasses and many other teases. Don't forget, if you're not happy with the answer go somewhere else. There are many options to consider, not least Oddbins.

Big parties at home

The key to a good party is keeping everyone happy and, while at a small dinner party you can afford to be a little experimental, at larger parties you are less 'in control' so every effort should be made to ensure simplicity. You should enjoy the evening too.

Try to appeal to the greater audience rather than following your own love and giving a Tequila Mezcal with a worm to every guest. This does not mean that you have to be boring, just don't be too clever! Beer and a range of spirits are always useful (gin, whisky, etc) but if you want to keep things simple, don't offer too much choice to start with, otherwise you will be running around mixing Martinis when you want to be talking to your guests.

Remember that you call the shots. If you don't mind mixing lots of different drinks or if you have some helpers, that's great. However, if you don't want to be doing that, then just offer wine and beer and leave it at that. Your guests will soon let you know if they want something else so, if you can, make sure you have the cabinet full just in case!

WINE

The latter half of this century has seen a worldwide wine explosion, as more open global trading and advanced transport systems, together with better vineyard and winery management, have combined to bring a multitude of vinous treasures to the market. Britain has embraced this more than most because our 'wine culture' has always been quite international. We have always had to look abroad for much of our wine because of our temperamental climate. Historically, changing political allegiances, and the trade agreements or restrictions that they have created, have meant that no single country's wine has entirely dominated the British market. As a result, we are distinctly more adventurous than many and the Aladdin's Caves that are the wine merchants on Britain's High Streets offer some of the best lists in the world.

courtesy of Dennis Ramsey

However, the flip side of this is that the sheer number of wines now available makes the job of actually choosing your wines that much more difficult! It seems that new wines from new regions and producers appear on the shelves each day. When faced with a sea of unknown names, there are, unfortunately, no hard and fast rules to ensure that you pick the perfect wine each time. Don't despair, however, as there is (or should be) help at hand to help you sort through the maze of labels in front of you.

- Always go to a merchant you know and trust. You can rely on them having done the initial leg work and having selected only good wines to start with! Even if the wine doesn't end up being a favourite, you will at least know that it's a good wine.

- Whenever possible ask for advice in the shop. The assistant should know a great many of (if not all!) the wines in his or her shop and so is well placed to advise you. Don't be shy as that's what they are there for. It will not be seen as your not knowing about wine, it will be seen as your showing an interest in what you are about to buy.

- Even an 'expert' would find it impossible to know exactly what a wine will taste like if they've never tried it before - they can only guess too! The only way to really know is to taste the wine, and many merchants offer free in-store tastings of selected wines. This is a good way to try before you buy but if this is not possible, then purchase a couple of bottles and try them out at home - it can always be an excuse for a smaller get-together.

HOW MUCH?

The amount of wine to get is always a tricky one as everybody's parties are different! You know your guests and also how long you want them to stay so, depending upon whether it's a quiet drink or a full blown celebration, you will need to give as much detail as possible to your merchant. Whatever the case, always have a little more than you need. There is nothing worse than running out and having to steal away to the nearest off-licence, praying it is still open, to get in more supplies. Most merchants will offer a sale or return service on larger orders, so enquire about this and, if you can, take advantage of it. You can't lose out.

courtesy of Searcy's & Joanna Plumbe Photography

'Plenty to drink' includes water and soft drinks. These are often an afterthought but are extremely important to a successful party. Some people will be driving and others simply do not drink very much, some not at all. These guests are as much a part of the party as the rest so don't forget them and maybe find something a little more interesting than water!

With regard to the wine, a 50/50 mix of white and red is a good bet. More and more people are drinking red wine these days as doctors announce that (in moderation) it is good for us. If you are starting with fizz, many people prefer to go on to red afterwards, another reason to keep the balance more even than has perhaps been traditionally recommended for parties. A party on a hot summer's evening will, of course, call for more refreshing white wines and beers. Ask for some advice so that the quantities can be tailored to your individual needs.

A VERY ROUGH GUIDE (BASED ON 6 GLASSES TO A BOTTLE)

If it's just drinks (cocktails) from 6-8pm

If it's just drinks and you want everyone to leave by, say, 8pm, half a bottle per head will be ample. Not everyone will be drinking so this will cover you with some to spare. However, if you really do want everyone to leave at a certain time, do not have all the drinks out on show. As long as it is there people will keep drinking and stay on, so if time is of the essence, keep some of the bottles hidden away!

If it's a birthday party from 7.30pm

It is becoming the 'norm' for people to bring a bottle along to this kind of party and, although this can be a significant boost to your supplies, it cannot be guaranteed. You should still order the full quota but remember the sale or return service - you needn't be saddled with lots of bottles you don't want. A bottle and a half per head is a rough figure to work on.

Look out for bulk discounts - most merchants will offer a case discount on wine and champagnes often attract special discounts such as 15 for the price of 12.

DRIVERS

Whenever you can, encourage your friends not to drive in the first place. 0800 654321 taxi number is always useful in the UK as this offers a virtually nationwide service. This number automatically connects you to the nearest taxi firm, wherever you are in the country. No more scrabbling through the Yellow Pages at 3 o'clock in the morning!

GLASSES

Many merchants offer a glass loan or hire service free if the wine is purchased from their shop. If you do not have caterers who can supply you with glasses, then take advantage of this service. It not only means you will have plenty of glasses, but you will also avoid breaking your best crystal. A few pounds paid for some broken/missing hired glasses is better than £20 a glass to replace a precious wedding present.

DELIVERY

Good merchants will offer delivery. This can be arranged to suit you, so, if you do not want the wine until the morning of the event, just let them know. Not everyone will collect (glasses or leftover wine) afterwards so remember to check when arranging the delivery in case this causes any problems for you the next day.

ICE - CHILLING YOUR DRINKS

Again, many merchants will sell ice. To chill down white wines, champagne and beers successfully use a dustbin (or the bath if it is convenient to get to during the party). Don't fill it with ice but use about one third ice to two thirds water. The cold water surrounds the bottles more quickly than ice on its own. Keep plenty of ice in the freezer for gin and tonics and soft drinks. A lukewarm orange juice will not impress the non-drinkers amongst your guests! In the winter you can keep your stores outside. The drinks will chill as well as in a fridge and everything can be chilled together, so no need to remember to keep replenishing stocks taken from the fridge.

CORKSCREWS/OPENERS

A seemingly obvious suggestion but they go walkabout very easily as people pick them up and take them out to the garden and so on. There is nothing more annoying (or frustrating) than having nothing to open the bottles with!

RISK MANAGEMENT

Roll back any treasured rugs and cover any pale coloured furniture. This is more to do with the number of people than any suggestion that your guests may drink too much! People will always put glasses on the floor or on the edge of a table and, if the room is crowded, people simply won't see the glass there and will knock it over.

At the end of it all, you should also enjoy the party too, so don't make any more work for yourself than is necessary!

Karen Wise, Oddbins

The black and white party that I referred to earlier was a winner for another reason - the host and hostess used the marquee and its effects four times in the week whilst the edifice and all its splendid happenings were in place. He was a farmer, she a marvellous hostess in a typically gracious way. The farm workers, the village inhabitants, business acquaintances were entertained prior to the main event - the host's 50th birthday. There were different themes for each occasion, a varied menu was introduced to each evening and they were all winners! While much of this may be down to the bonhomie of the hosts, the effort put in enabled far more to be entertained in a truly memorable setting.

While considerable expense was incurred, the whole budget was apportioned and, knowing my friend, written off as a business expense!

Some are remarkably good at managing space successfully, others are appalling - the golden rule, surely, is if in doubt be generous - people don't like a squash (unless of course its a student's/youngster's party when unless you are cramped like sardines the event is a non-starter). People by and large enjoy space - don't go over the top and jeopardise the atmosphere but use your space wisely. Plan in advance a good place for the coats - so you don't have a coat orgy at the end of the evening. Ensure that there is plenty of loo paper, soap, towels etc. Pretty basic really but still easy to overlook.

Space

Here are a few golden rules:

- Allow 6 square feet per person for a cocktail reception with no occasional furniture
- Allow 12 square feet per person for a seated, served dinner
- Allow 15 square feet per person for a seated buffet

If the above seems wrong, try it for yourself. Pace out a square yard (one big stride in four directions to form a square). Be totally strict about the size. Don't alter or fudge it. The square should be three feet on each side.

Next get a few friends to help you. If two of you can stand comfortably in this square, you've allowed yourselves 4.5 square feet per person. If you want the party packed, then three of you should try and stand in this square. Now try imitating eating and drinking actions without breaking out of the square, and without knocking your friends over.

Freddie Meynell, Searcy's

courtesy of Dennis Ramsey

Equipment for a large party

To illustrate the types and quantities of equipment required for a party, Gorgeous Gourmets have calculated what is needed for a seated wedding lunch for 100.

Before you even start thinking about what equipment to order, you need to ask yourself a few questions:

What are you serving for lunch? How many courses? How many of those are hot? How many wines are you serving? Are you serving champagne for toasts? Are you serving port and liqueurs?

You cannot order so much as a teaspoon before deciding on a menu and how the food will be served. For this example, we will imagine that you have chosen a three-course meal: smoked salmon with bread and butter (pre-plated), a hot main course with three vegetables, a pudding (pre-plated), followed by coffee. White and red wines will be served with the meal, champagne with the dessert and the toasts.

Each person will need:

Starter:	Small knife, small fork, starter plate (8in)
Bread & butter:	Small knife, side plate (6in)
Main:	Large knife, large fork, dinner plate (10in)
Pudding:	Dessert spoon, dessert fork, dessert bowl or plate (8in)
Coffee:	Coffee cup and saucer, coffee spoon
Glasses:	Water (12oz), red wine (8oz), white wine (6oz), champagne flutes

(If you can, try to use the same shaped glasses throughout - in other words use a water goblet rather than a tumbler. It makes the table look much prettier.)

Assuming you are having silver service, each table will require: serving dishes for all three courses, including platters for the main course, vegetable dishes, and serving spoons and forks. Depending on your menu, you may need gravy and/or sauce boats.

Every table will also need salts and peppers (probably two sets per table), butter dishes, milk/cream jugs and sugar bowls, cafétières or coffee pots, and ashtrays for the smokers.

Total equipment requirement would then be:

	Per Person	For 100
China	1 x 10" plate	100
	2 x 8" plates	200
	1 x 6" plate	100
	1 x coffee cup/saucer	100
Cutlery:	1 x large knife	100
	1 x large fork	100
	2 x small knives	200
	2 x small fork	200
	1 x dessert spoon	100
	1 x coffee spoon	100
Glasses:	1 x 12oz (water)	100
	1 x 8oz (red wine)	100
	1 x 6oz (white wine)	100
	champagne flute	100

	Per Table	Total
	2 x salt & pepper	24
	1 x sauce boat	12
	1 x bread-basket	12
	1 x butter dish	12
	1 x milk jug	12

Per Table	Total
1 x sugar bowl	12
1 x cafétière / pot	12

Serving dishes

1 x main course	12
3 x vegetable	36
4 x serving tools	48
1 x serving tray	12

Make certain you have enough trays for clearing away (after the guests have gone) as well as service cloths, tea towels, etc.

If the food is being laid out buffet-style, then you will need different types of serving equipment such as chafing dishes, large serving platters, etc, as well as serving spoons and forks.

Now you need to think about adding table linen to the hire list. You can hire a wide range of linen, in an array of materials, colours and sizes. Whether you are tying the colours in with the marquee lining or the colours of the bride's flowers, do get swatches from the hire company to avoid last minute panics.

If you are having a hot lunch, there are further elements that you must consider. If your wedding lunch is taking place in a marquee with no access to kitchen facilities, you might need to bring in some type of heating equipment. This may be as simple as chafing dishes, or could be turbo or microwave ovens, gas or electric ranges, Baby Bellings, etc and you would almost certainly need some types of refrigeration. Will there be access to mains power or will you have to use a generator or bottled gas, or a combination?

In the winter (and in the spring and the autumn in England, to be on the safe side!) heating should be provided. And then there is the question of washroom facilities. Do you want one hundred guests using the loos in your house? Can your plumbing system cope with it?

Amanda Stephenson, Gorgeous Gourmets

courtesy of Searcy's & Joanna Plumbe Photography

Make the most of marquees

Customers tell us that they have chosen a marquee setting for a number of reasons. Marquees are personal and can be tailored to your exact size and decor requirements. Marquee celebrations achieve major cost savings in the areas of food and drink compared to hotel or restaurant prices. Marquees provide an instant celebratory atmosphere and underline the feeling of occasion and exclusivity.

SIZE

The first question asked by any potential customer is "what size marquee do I need?". In this section we will try to provide some answers, although every event is different in some special way and every client will have personal preferences. The space available will also have a bearing on the marquee choice.

If you are using round tables, the 'rule of thumb' is to allow 15 sq ft or approximately 1.5 sq m per guest. This allows comfortable dining space for your guests and sufficient space for the waiting staff to move freely amongst the tables. Dance floors (allow approximately 3 sq ft per guest) and stage areas must also be considered together with plenty of room in front of bar and buffet areas. The following chart gives a rough guide to sizes.

| | Approximate Number of Guests | |
Marquee Size	Finger Buffet	Dining at Table
9 x 9m (30 x 30ft)	100	60
9 x 12m (30 x 45ft)	150	90
9 x 18m (30 x 60ft)	200	120
9 x 24m (30 x 75ft)	250	150
9 x 27m (30 x 90ft)	300	180
12 x 10m (40 x 33ft)	150	90
12 x 15m (40 x 50ft)	220	130
12 x 20m (40 x 66ft)	280	170
12 x 25m (40 x 83ft)	350	210
12 x 30m (40 x 100ft)	430	260
12 x 35m (40 x 116ft)	500	300
12 x 40m (40 x 133ft)	580	350

Remember to add space for reception areas, bar areas and dance floors, many of which can be added on successfully as connected alcoves.

Table Size	Informal/Buffet Barbeque/Hog Roast	Formal/Banquet Silver Service
4ft Round	8	6
5ft Round	10	8
6ft Round	12	10

Don't forget that by specifying a lower number of guests per table you will automatically increase the marquee size required and therefore add to your bill!

LAYOUTS

There are a few "golden rules" to observe, otherwise it's your party.

* Although the marquee contractor will provide an initial plan in consultation with you, make sure your caterer agrees. They have to work in it, after all!

* Try to give your caterer easy access to the kitchen tent for refrigerated vehicles and position the kitchen for ease of access to buffet points or bars.

* Keep bars well away from dance floors.

* If you have mobile loo units supplied, remember to provide an awning for access/waiting at peak usage times.

- If your marquee is a long distance from your house or from the car park, you may be faced with a huge bill for walkway roofs. A stylish and cost-saving alternative is to equip some young (good looking!) volunteers with carriage umbrellas to escort guests to the marquee! The fun begins here!

- Never place a disco on a dance floor. They must be on a separate surface so dancers don't disturb equipment and distort sound.

- In winter remember to allow space in heated marquees for garment rails and cloakrooms near the entrance.

Have a marvellous time!

Stephen Keyes, The Marquee Company

Put plainly, although marquees might look pretty, there are numerous pitfalls above and below the ground, not to mention the massive amount of consideration one must give to the weather. One essential piece of advice, as that rather ghastly travel agent used to say, is "book early".

Although a good marquee company can provide many of the trappings associated with a marquee - lining, flooring, furniture, heating, etc, there are a whole range of other exciting additions you can consider. As with most things in life, it is your imagination as much as your budget that can make all the difference.

Decorating marquees

Traditional marquees or the larger aluminium framed temporary structures are being used more and more for large events. The advantage is that the size and shape can be changed to suit the numbers and the event. The disadvantage is that they are often barn-like and require creative decoration. It makes an interesting challenge for the floral decorator, rather like painting on a blank canvas - although it is more likely to be PVC these days! Here the specialist decorator comes into his or her own. Large trees and palms up to 5m high really look spectacular inside these structures and guests cannot believe how on earth you managed to get them in.

courtesy of Searcy's & Joanna Plumbe Photography

Marquees are often located in fields or car parks, which can look very uninviting from the outside. It is important for the floral designer to look at the overall design of the area outside at an early stage in the planning. Pathways, screen fencing, gardens and water features are the armoury of event landscape companies and can transform an unattractive car park into the hanging gardens of Babylon within hours. A fountain, rock waterfall or feature garden area can create interest and perhaps a focal point to take the eye away from less attractive areas.

Above all, floral design is about creating an interesting and stimulating environment - have fun with it!

Andy Metcalf, Expo Flora Ltd

Light can be the most wonderful thing but we take it for granted too much. We often assume that it's like some faithful old Labrador - always there. Well, today light is readily accessible but in a marquee situation extra thought needs to be taken to avoid practical problems. If used to good effect, lighting can make a marquee that much more special. There is something wonderfully romantic about carefully lit flower beds or walkways, and there are the practical aspects of showing the way to weary revellers.

To me, however, there is one kind of light that is inextricably linked to the marquee situation . . . that is, of course, the sunrise breaking at dawn. And that is impossible to engineer no matter how good the lighting engineer may be.

Lighting in a marquee

Marquees are like beginning a novel with a blank sheet of paper - here is a space, four walls and a ceiling with no facilities inside whatsoever. Admittedly there will be a brief to follow: so many tables, a band stage and a dance floor, a reception area, decor and floral features - all of which require lights. Equally, 'backstage' there will be kitchen areas, toilets, access and safety elements - all of these will need attention. With so much space, options for lighting are legion. The question becomes "How much will your budget stand?" With today's aluminium structures it is possible to hang a lot of weight in a marquee roof, so you just have to decide when to stop.

Traditionally a marquee would be put up and the lighting would be simple: chandeliers and wall brackets. The objective was to create an ambient light level that would allow people to see where they were going, what they were doing and what they were eating. They might appreciate the ability to have this level dimmed down for dinner, relying on the soft-glow of table candles to provide a more intimate atmosphere. Today a basic lighting scheme would include spotlights to table centres and uplighting the walls and bouncing off the roof lining so that an indirect ambient light level is created. From here one may build a lighting scheme which is both effective and functional by focusing spotlights onto other elements of the party. If there are flower arrangements—light them, bring out the colour, make the most of their statement. Buffets or bars—light them . . . if you don't you'll leave the functional areas in darkness, which is neither practical nor inviting. The picture will appear incomplete.

A point that arises many times when planning an event is that any areas missed out of the lighting scheme will be in relative darkness. Remember if you have arranged for small floral arrangements on occasional tables in a reception area their impact will be vastly reduced if they are in shadow for the evening. On a practical note - don't forget to allow for lighting in the service areas, the kitchens, cloakrooms etc. Bear in mind also that while most of your

courtesy of Fisher

guests may arrive in daylight, they will be leaving after dark. Access lighting can be important also for those working on after the evening is over.

One great advantage of a marquee over most other venues is that you are presented with a choice as to the colour of the walls and ceiling—they do not have to be plain white. Aside from colour options, there is the popular option of a 'starcloth' roof so the ceiling becomes a night sky of stars. Obviously, the selection of coloured linings will have a bearing upon lighting plans. With starcloth the golden rule is to keep direct light off the black material. Shine a light at the roof and you will see the material and completely lose the magic effect. Create the ambient level with downlights.

Another interesting effect in marquees is to place lights behind the lining, as the lightweight material is ideal for diffusing light sources. One example of this would be to place coloured floodlights up in the roof. These can be used to create a welcoming atmosphere when the guests first arrive, and then one could mix or change to other colours: pale sunshine gold for the early evening changing to dark midnight blue for the duration of the meal and after dinner dancing etc. Given the vagaries of the British weather, placing floodlights behind the lining offers a controllable means of guaranteeing a bright cheerful environment even if the sun is obviously absent. Marquees are, by definition, areas shaded from natural light so it is quite common to light them even for lunches. If the sun shines brightly your effects may be invalidated, but some occasions require the belt and braces approach to be on the safe side.

With the rigging opportunities offered in a marquee one is able to be selective with the lighting. For dance floors and bands, all the effects and moving lights can be installed directly overhead so the impact is felt exactly where it is aimed, at the dancers, rather than intruding throughout the tent - though the range of the music may be less restricted!

Bear in mind that marquees can be fitted with windows anywhere you might wish, so you might consider exterior lighting offering an after-dark perspective of trees or landscapes. Equally the marquee may be built over features of the garden. Don't leave these out - if you've got them, flaunt them.

courtesy of Searcy's & Joanna Plumbe Photography

courtesy of Dennis Ramsey

Fisher

It's one problem clearing up after a small party but dealing with a bigger affair is a different matter - it's all hands on and if you can enlist the support of a few cleaner uppers first thing the next morning, then that's a great idea. It may be that your caterers have agreed to undertake such work and, if so, well done but don't overlook it or the perfect party will really turn into the complete nightmare.

The aftermath of a big event can be so depressing - the party went swimmingly, the bride looked beautiful, the best man didn't mention 'that story', but what are we going to do now? Well, probably the best thing to do is have a few days away - maybe then mother nature will have brought your delightful garden back to its former glory!

The grass is never greener

This is a simple statement of fact, understood by anyone who has ever hosted a party under canvas on their own lawn. Once the men have dismantled the marquee and left for the next party, your personal piece of England will have been transformed. This is not, however, a design miracle brought about by the likes of Alan Titchmarsh. I am talking about a change in colour scheme from verdant swathe to jaundiced pallor that is visible from outer space. Once-proud manicured lawn, boasting parallel stripes, takes on the appearance of a sun-starved patch, crying out for fresh chlorophyll.

If you have been particularly unlucky, and enjoyed a period of wet weather before your event, you will also have some other new features to admire:

courtesy of Grimsthorpe Castle

•The vehicle that delivered your temporary generator will have left several deep, grass-free ruts. Standing proud, like razor-slash scars on the face of a Chicago gangster, they will remain with you all year unless some drastic action is taken to flatten, aerate and reseed them.

•The caterers will have emptied their pans of boiling water just outside the marquee and the par-boiled grass, now totally devoid of life, will have turned brown overnight. Brown polka-dot lawns have yet to become fashionable.

•The band, in their hurry to leave to catch the last decent bacon sandwiches at the motorway café, will have driven at speed across the grass. Their figure-of-eight manoeuvres (executed whilst they determined which was the real way out from your property) will have produced superb wheel-spin marks on the damp herbage, and the blackened, torn fragments of grass bear testimony to the fact that 1979 Ford transit vans do have double sets of wheels on their rear axles.

•The portaloos may have been collected but their location will be denoted by the muddy trail from the site of the marquee. The presence of a solitary black stiletto indicates that this was a formal evening.

Once you have scoured the area and collected all the champagne corks, cigarette ends, soggy place-setting cards, crushed button-holes and the dozens of six-inch long pieces of electrical tape that are essential to the success of any outdoor event, you can relax, safe in the knowledge that within three weeks you will never know that 300 people danced the night away on your lawn. Except, that is, when you get a phone call from a friend of a friend who wonders if they can hold a ball at your place because someone they knew had such a fantastic time there last month . . .

Ray Biggs, Grimsthorpe Castle

So, after the marquee has gone and the garden's repaired, or the site empty where formerly thousands trod . . . what's next? Well, there's always next time, if you can face it! Hopefully the information in this chapter will ensure that the success you so rightly deserve comes to fruition . . . here are a few reminders.

Checklist for marquee events

- ☐ Locate a venue with a suitable site
- ☐ Arrange a meeting to discuss the marquee and other facilities

With your supplier's help, establish the following:

- ☐ A layout plan for the site
- ☐ Does the site have suitable access for large vehicles/fire tenders
- ☐ Are there any restrictions to working hours?
- ☐ Are there sufficient parking facilities?
- ☐ Is the site level and well drained?
- ☐ Is the site clear of underground and/or overhead obstructions?
- ☐ Is a suitable power supply available?
- ☐ Is a water supply available for caterers and toilet facilities?
- ☐ Is there a facility for waste water and refuse disposal?
- ☐ Are there suitable facilities for disabled guests?
- ☐ Inform local authorities, i.e. Health and Safety/Fire Officer as necessary
- ☐ Obtain necessary licences
- ☐ Order marquee and furnishings
- ☐ Choose a caterer
- ☐ Arrange lighting - internal/external
- ☐ Power supply/generator
- ☐ Temporary toilet facilities
- ☐ Security of the site
- ☐ Security staff
- ☐ Cleaners pre event/during event
- ☐ First aid
- ☐ Fire fighting equipment

Safety and fire precautions

- ☐ Telephone (to call emergency services)
- ☐ Access to hydrants and other water supplies should not be obstructed or obscured
- ☐ No dangerous, combustible or toxic gases or other allied products such as aerosols, explosives or pyrotechnics should be stored within a tented structure
- ☐ Very few tented structures have snow load capacity and if snow is a possibility the structure must be heated in order to maintain a minimum temperature of 12°C to prevent build-up of snow on the roof
- ☐ The area beneath stages, platforms, etc should not be used for storage
- ☐ Exit routes should be kept free from obstruction at all times

Other things to think about

- ☐ Event insurance
- ☐ Car park attendants
- ☐ Crowd control marshals
- ☐ Site office
- ☐ On site communications
- ☐ Public address system
- ☐ Site signage
- ☐ Invitations
- ☐ Provide location map for guests
- ☐ Flowers
- ☐ Table plans
- ☐ MC/Toastmaster
- ☐ Entertainment
- ☐ Have I complied with the statutory regulations on Health and Safety and Fire Authority
- ☐ Site cleaning and reinstatement of site
- ☐ Return all small hired items such as communication systems
- ☐ Last check on site
- ☐ Keep accurate records and notes for future reference

STANDARD CAPACITIES FOR MARQUEES

Key:

A = Presentation with chairs in rows only, including gangways
B = Dining only at round tables with silver service
C = Reception area, dining at round tables with silver service and dancing

Frame Tent Size W x L Metres	M²	Ft²	Persons			Heating Requirements kw's per hour	Cooling Requirements kw's per hour
			A	B	C		
12 x 20	240	2583	350	160	110	140	50
12 x 25	300	3229	430	200	135	175	60
12 x 30	360	3875	520	240	160	230	65
16 x 20	320	3444	460	220	140	175	60
16 x 25	400	4305	580	270	180	260	75
16 x 30	480	5166	690	320	215	260	100
16 x 35	560	6027	800	380	250	350	100
16 x 40	640	6888	920	430	290	375	125
20 x 25	500	5381	720	340	230	260	100
20 x 30	600	6458	860	400	270	350	125
20 x 40	800	8611	1150	540	360	520	150
24 x 30	720	7750	1030	480	320	465	145
24 x 40	960	10333	1380	640	430	520	200
24 x 50	1200	12916	1720	800	540	700	250
24 x 60	1440	15500	2060	960	640	864	300
24 x 70	1680	18083	2400	1120	750	1050	350
24 x 80	1920	20666	2750	1280	860	1050	400
40 x 40	1600	17222	2290	1070	720	960	320
40 x 60	2400	25833	3430	1600	1070	1515	500
40 x 80	3200	34444	4580	2140	1430	1920	640

Note 1 Kw = 3412 BTU's per hour

The figures given are averages taken from countless successfully completed contracts. When ordering, individual tastes, table sizes, layout and weather conditions should be taken into consideration.

Heating and cooling
Whilst all skill and reasonable care have been taken to determine accurate estimations, ambient conditions do vary from month to month and year to year and from location to location within the UK. The use of these figures therefore is for guidelines only.

Bill Preston, Owen Brown Ltd

At Home

The principal advantage of entertaining at home can be summed up by considering the two Cs: cost and convenience. There's probably a third C but I can't think of it right now. Anyway, whether you're entertaining on a budget or with no financial cares in the world, your home is your castle (is that C number three?) and within it you can do just about anything. What follows is a veritable array of ideas to turn your dreams into reality.

There are all manner of tricks you can try. Like everything else, food and drink can be made dull or, with a little thought, special. I can remember on one Valentine's Day being offered a plate of five Chinese delights at the centre of which was a beautifully carved carrot. It looked so tempting that I picked it up and thrust it into my mouth. I had just swallowed the end when I realised from the faces around me that I had eaten a willy . . . yes, you can do a lot with food!

Making your party a success

Parties start and end with guests. Sometimes putting together a disparate cocktail of people works and sometimes it's a disaster. Whatever happens, your success rate is greatly improved if you introduce people - an old-fashioned concept which is too often forgotten.

- Make a list with your guests' names with a one liner about each one and pin it next to the loo. This acts as a great aide memoire.

- At the beginning work out your budget. There is nothing more disappointing than having wonderful ideas and finding you can't afford them. Nowhere is it more important to 'cut your coat', than with entertaining. It's better to serve a decent wine than cheap champagne, sausage and mash than poor quality caviar.

- Busy parties are fun, crowded parties are hell.

- Music should never be so loud that you can't hear somebody speak.

- Get the local printer to print the invitations but buy the envelopes from a luxury stationer.

- If you are employing caterers, try the food before you hire them.

- Never stint on waiting staff. People notice empty glasses and poor service.

- Make the house or wherever you are holding your party smell wonderful. Jo Malone's room scents are the best.

- If you are erecting a marquee, make sure the walls are at least 3 metres high. There is nothing more embarrassing than a speech-making bridegroom with his head inside the tent ceiling lining.

- At weddings always have more canapés than you could possibly need. Most of your guests won't have had lunch and the bride and groom's male friends will still have appetites like horses.

- Always see mobile loos before you confirm the booking. The description in the brochure may be different from the reality.

- Make sure the matting/carpeting in marquees is carefully laid. A grandmother falling over at a wedding can ruin the day.

- Fence off swimming pools, especially if there are young bridesmaids and pages.

- Never have glasses round a swimming pool. The early morning dive the day after a party would take on a whole new dimension with a tumbler in your head.

- Be methodical about monitoring replies. It is embarrassing when two extra guests suddenly appear for dinner.

- Unless you are very rich, it makes sense to use flowers that are in season, but never be frightened to use unpromising domestic containers - galvanised zinc, plastic washing-up bowls, even a dustpan and brush.

- Fireworks in birthday cakes look great in pictures, in reality they often cover the cake with fine black dust.

- Buy lots of ice.

- Don't make cocktails too strong - your guests are there to have fun, not sleep.

- Make time for yourself to relax and chill out before your guests arrive - they will relax if you are relaxed.

- Make sure you have fresh orange juice and a decent supply of coffee for the following morning.

Rolline Frewen, The Admirable Crichton

Although the company occasion or big party can be wonderful, the majority of entertaining is done at home and usually in a far more modest way. Assuming, however, that one wishes to push the old boat out, there are numerous devices that can be tried at home without causing a disaster. This is not a chapter about keeping up with the Joneses (well, it is a bit!). No, its main intention is to give a few hints from real professionals on how to maximise the impact of an occasion without necessarily having to spend a fortune.

courtesy of Searcy's & Joanna Plumbe Photography

Quid te exempta iuvat spinis de pluribus una?
Vivere si recte nescis, decede peritis.
Lusisti satis, edisti satis atque bibisti:
Tempus abire tibi est.

What pleasure does it give to be rid of one thorn out of
   many? If you don't know how to live right, give
   way to those who are expert at it. You have had
   enough fun, eaten and drunk enough: time you were
   off.

Horace

While there is potential for disaster at every turn in running any occasion, there are some areas less complex than others, and if you follow some basic rules when choosing your wine this is an area that can be dealt with efficiently. But like most of life's more straightforward preoccupations wine is often taken for granted. Here are a few thoughts from a master of his trade.

How to choose wine for a party

In order to throw a really good party you have to be totally confident with what you are serving. If you could only cook one dish really well, would you consider hosting regular dinner parties? I don't think so. Yet it is surprising how many people entertain and expect you to drink the same wine every time.

If you are a person with a grand repertoire of just one or two wines I urge you to start trying different styles of wines as soon as possible so that you can serve them with panache. For a fair chance of success, never serve something you have not tried, and enjoyed beforehand yourself. Experiment and widen your horizons, but on your own first. Never treat party guests as guinea pigs.

Apart from getting to know what is available from your local supermarket, try to find a good wine merchant or two in your area. As with a hairdresser, describe what you want in detail and see how good they are at interpreting your needs. A great wine merchant is a Godsend in times of panic and indecision.

When it comes to choosing a wine for a particular party the first question to ask is "how much money is available?" A depressingly frequent sentence I hear which never ceases to send a shudder of horror down my spine is "We'll get . . . X . . . because it is dirt cheap and no-one will know the difference." PLEASE! On no account choose the cheapest wine available unless you really enjoy drinking it yourself. If you want to serve wine, but can't afford to be too generous, buy a bottle or two of good wine and make it into a long drink. Add plenty of lemonade or sparkling water, ice and fruit to white wine or a light red in summer or warm some red wine up in winter with plenty of water, a reasonable amount of sugar, spices such as cinnamon and nutmeg and add a few oranges studded with cloves. Experiment with various recipes until you hit on one or two really successful ones.

On the other hand, even if you have an incredibly handsome wine budget, don't choose great old wines unless you know that you and all your guests will appreciate them. I don't mean by this that they are too good for the plebs, but older 'fine' wines need more knowledge and experience to appreciate: they are an acquired taste. They may well increase in subtle secondary flavours and their bouquets usually become fascinating but their power definitely diminishes. A person used to drinking block-busting Shiraz from Australia will quite likely be disappointed with such wines although if they know you spent a fortune on them they may not let on.

This brings me to another important point - do you know your guests and their tastes, or are they relative strangers? If you know specific favourite wines - or perhaps allergies - try to accommodate them. Try to make each guest feel special.

So much for generalities, now what about some definite suggestions? First of all, if you are planning a drinks party with just a few nibbles to eat, may I suggest you go for the more full flavoured, single grape variety wines from Australia, New Zealand, California or South America - Chardonnay and/or Sauvignon Blanc for white and Cabernet Sauvignon, Merlot or Shiraz for red. They are delicious on their own, great value for money and almost universally popular. Don't forget to to have a bottle or two of medium sweet white, such as German 'Kabinett' or 'Spätlese', for those with a sweeter tooth and, although we are talking about the wine, please remember to have plenty of water and soft drinks available. Surprising as it may seem, not everyone wants to drink alcohol all day or night long.

When it comes to choosing wines for luncheons or dinner parties the fun really begins. To get a good idea of what wine will go with a dish I try to think of it as an accompaniment or condiment rather than a drink in its own right. For example, if you served a grilled dover sole, would you prefer it with a squeeze of lemon juice or a spoonful of sugar: a crisp, dry Chablis, or a sweet Sauternes? I hope your answer, unless you are perverse, was the lemon/Chablis. If you turn fish into a curry however the question is still simple but the answer is more open to personal taste. It depends whether you prefer yogurt with your curry or mango chutney, raisins, coconut and banana.

What follow now are a few combinations that I have particularly enjoyed in the past, and included so that you can decide whether to try some of my ideas or write me off as an idiot.

Dish: Charcoal grilled lamb cutlets, chips and a crisp green salad
Wine: A big red Rioja
Note: The rich red fruit and oaky flavours of the wine marry beautifully with the smoky taste of the sweetish meat. Also try Australian or Californian Pinot Noir

Dish: Goat's cheese - either plain after a meal or toasted on a salad as a starter
Wine: Any Sauvignon Blanc, Sancerre, Pouilly Fumé or New Zealand Sauvignon Blanc
Note: Although one usually eats a mouthful of food and then takes a sip of wine, try keeping both in your mouth at the same time and, after you swallow them, breathe out through your nose keeping your mouth shut. If you don't choke, I think you will find the flavour of the cheese and wine harmonise incredibly well and float around in the back of your nose. NB. only try this in private as it can be messy - but it does help me to discover really great marriages of food and wine

Dish: Poached salmon (hot or cold), boiled potatoes and salad
Wine: Chablis
Note: Again a great combination. The clean dry quality of the wine enhances the taste of the salmon. On the whole I prefer to match white wine with fish but if you like red wine poach a piece of salmon in a little Beaujolais and serve it with the rest of the wine.

After a heavy meal experiment with a very chilled glass of Asti Spumanti but hide the bottle in the kitchen and serve it already in the glass - a disparaging remark from a wine snob can put the whole room off the wine. The light fruitiness of Asti, however, is especially refreshing after a large meal and it often partners the dessert much more successfully than a solid Sauternes or Muscat de Beaumes de Venise.

Please note that all these are only suggestions and far from being the only wines I would choose for these dishes.

HOW TO KEEP WINE, WELL

Perhaps it is worth mentioning here that you don't need the perfect cellar or any storage space at all to throw even a large party. Most wine merchants will be willing to keep your order for a day or two, especially if you pay when you order. If you really want to start a cellar of your own and don't have any space at home there are also merchants who rent out part of their own cellars for private customers' stock.

If you are going to keep wine at home for more than a day or two, however, there are certain things to watch and temperature is probably the most important. Wherever you decide to keep wine you should have as constant a temperature as possible. Constant heating up and cooling down definitely changes the flavour of the wine for the worse. As far as the actual temperature is concerned, the ideal is somewhere about 9 -12 degrees centigrade, but if you have no thermometer just feel the bottles regularly. If they feel neutral to cool you've gauged things pretty well. If the bottles feel slightly warm or hot move them to a cooler place and more unlikely, if they feel very cold move them to a slightly warmer place.

Another important point to watch when storing wine is that all the bottles are kept horizontal rather than vertical. This ensures that the cork stays in contact with the wine and keeps moist and elastic. If the bottle is kept standing up the cork eventually dries out and shrinks enabling air to enter the bottle and so spoil the wine.

The storage area doesn't have to be very dark, but very bright light or direct sunlight will, apart from heating up the wine, affect the colour as it does that of a carpet or wallpaper. Two more minor considerations are that the area is free from excessive vibration and any very pervasive smells.

From this it can be seen that the cupboard under the stairs is usually good enough unless there are hot pipes running through it or a family of little elephants are regularly using the stairs for trampoline practice.

If you intend to serve more than one or two bottles of white wine, unless you have a massive, under-used fridge, you are going to need plenty of ice so don't forget to make some and freeze it - a tedious, time-consuming job - or order some from your local off licence.

White wines should be served between about 6-12 degrees centigrade, with the sweeter wines and sparkling wines at the cooler end of the scale and full-bodied, great white Burgundies at the higher end. In all my years of serving wine, I have now and again been told a red wine was too warm but rarely that a white was too cold. May I suggest that, unless you are serving the very finest wines, you put all the bottles you need in a big bucket or plastic dustbin and add plenty of ice and cold water about an hour before they are needed, making sure most of the necks are submerged.

courtesy of Masquerade

As far as red wine is concerned, bring the bottles into the room two or three hours before they are needed.

When opening a bottle of wine make sure that the capsule is neatly cut or removed completely and the neck is wiped if required. The cork should then be extracted as cleanly as possible. If the cork breaks don't panic. Get the large pieces out and strain the wine into a clean bottle or decanter using a funnel and coffee filter.

If you are serving old red wines that have a sediment it is necessary to decant them into clean glass decanters. The proper way to do this is to stand the bottle upright a day or two before the party so that the sediment falls to the bottom. Open the bottle carefully and pour gently in one action - traditionally using a candle behind the neck until you see the sediment approaching the top of the bottle and then stop. It is much easier, however, to cheat once again by using a coffee filter.

You must also check that all your glasses are spotlessly clean and you have enough of them to stop constantly washing up throughout the party. You may have to hire some extra glasses, in which case order a few extra get them a day or two early so you can check the boxes are not half empty, the glasses are clean and the rims are not chipped. If your party is to be a buffet or nibbles affair, it is also wise to expect a few breakages and lost glasses. It can be fascinating to see where and when the glasses reappear.

Finally the perfect host or hostess never lets the glasses run dry. If you have chosen your wines well guests will, fortunately or unfortunately, drink more. On the other hand he or she will never force a guest to drink another glass if they really don't want to.

Having said all this - whether your party is a roaring success or a howling disaster - remember the Golden Rule Number One:- Don't panic, relax. Pick up a glass of wine, sip it or slurp it, and, above all - enjoy yourself!

Cheers!

Michael Simms, Sommelier, The Savoy

While there may be two or three Cs, two Ps also leap readily to mind: Planning and Partying. The two are not always ideal bedfellows. Indeed, we've all surely enjoyed an evening which started with no particular pretence and developed into an evening to remember. There is nothing as marvellous as spontaneity, but as you can't rely on this rather elusive commodity, it is essential to revert to the more tiresome planning.

Most people only have a party (other than a dinner or supper party) once in a blue moon and it is therefore critical to make the most of it. As with everything, it is not just down to money. With a good imagination and some hard work even the drinks party (yawn) can become something to remember.

Small parties at home

Planning the small but perfect party at home is a difficult task for all discerning hosts. The guest list numbers around 30 - too big to be simply a few friends around for drinks or supper; too small to fall into the large party category. To many hosts, a party of 30 is likely to be one of the biggest, if not the biggest, party they give all year.

To complicate matters further, the party-givers are likely to be extremely busy running companies, managing careers or juggling jobs and families, so they have little time left to worry about the finer points of giving a party.

Before you reach for the headache tablets, fear not! Help is at hand in the form of professional party planners. To call them fairy Godmothers may seem a bit extreme, but with a wave of their 'magic wands' of efficiency and creativity they can take all

courtesy of Searcy's & Joanna Plumbe Photography

the pain out of party planning, leaving the hosts to enjoy the party. Don't make the mistake of feeling that your party is too small to be of interest to a party planner. Here are a few thoughts.

A word of advice about invitations. You should invite twenty-five percent more people than you expect to attend the party, particularly during the peak entertaining seasons of summer and Christmas. There will always be some who cannot attend. Such precautions save on the embarrassment of last minute invitations. Invitations should be sent out a month before the party, with an RSVP date of one week prior to the party. Reputable caterers do not require the final figures until three or four days beforehand as they will be buying their produce fresh and working around the hosts' requirements right up to the day before the event.

Having decided on a formal or informal theme, then the menu, drinks, balloons and other decorations and flowers may all be planned down to the last detail, always within the hosts' budgets.

If the party is to be held out of doors, gazebos would enhance the effect. Another option and highly recommended one, would be a 20' by 30' frame marquee with a 12' by 12' dance floor. This would meet all requirements and, by either leaving it open or closing it, would ensure a good party whatever the weather does!

When using the garden, take full advantage of its attractive or unusual features. If there is a topiary hedge, can it be incorporated as a divider between seating and dancing areas? The clever use of ground spike spotlights is extremely effective in illuminating garden features.

Focusing on specific themes here is not appropriate but a good planner will come up with brilliant ideas for the client to make their party unique and memorable. Ideas include straightforward theming (black and white, Mexican, etc) fancy dress, casino tables, magicians, balloon modellers, caricaturists, sketch artists, silhouettists or 'mix and mingle' characters from drunken waiters to fire performers or tarot card readers.

Entertainment will depend on the theme (and of course the budget!) but in general terms a band working solo or in conjunction with a disco is appropriate. Jazz is a popular option at the moment but the party planner will be able to recommend some other fun alternatives.

Don't forget the mundane, practical but highly important elements of parking, toilets and insurance. If you do not want to have everybody using the facilities in your house, 30 people can probably manage with one unisex portaloo. These are more efficient and certainly more attractive than they used to be, so don't be put off before you have investigated a little.

On the subject of parking, try to use the local school or, in rural areas, ask a farmer for the use of a field. Do think about setting some flares into the ground to light the way to the party and back again.

Party givers may need to take out insurance for an event on their premises and a quick call to your insurance company or broker is recommended.

courtesy of Elements Entertainments

Whatever the requirements, a party planner worth their salt will be able to fulfil them and save the hosts the stress so they enjoy their party as much as their guests.

Ruth Callard Rogers, Elements Events and Entertainments

Did ye not hear it?-No; 'twas the wind,
  Or the car rattling o'er the stony street;
On with the dance! let joy be unconfined;
  No sleep till the morn, when Youth and Pleasure meet
To chase the glowing Hours with flying feet.

Byron

It is important to consider many different ideas but never try to overdo it. Farlam Hall, like all Relais et Châteaux hotels and restaurants, excel at service when entertaining. Similarly, when entertaining at home similarly timing and service may make the difference between a fun evening and a nightmare in the kitchen, even if it is only a spare pair of hands for serving and washing up.

If you do think it's a good idea to hire some help for the evening - don't just dump them in the kitchen. When dinner is served ask them to make sure the area you might be having coffee in after dinner is looking fresh. Ask them to stoke up or light the fire, anything you would do yourself if you had the time. While many people may consider such niceties unimportant, if it's a special occasion why not make the effort–it will be less of a strain for you and your guests will love you forever. What follows are a few thoughts from a stately home run by one of the leading entertainers in the country.

A dinner party to delight in – or dread?

How often when you have done the deed - chosen the guests, the day and venue -does your heart sink, never to rise again until the last guest has vanished over the horizon? This need not be the case with some basic, advance planning - which should leave you time to enjoy everything - including a drink in the bath beforehand!

If you forget every other rule, remember just one thing. Never, ever, push your own house, or the chosen venue, into seating more people than you know, or have been told, the space can cope with. A crush at a cocktail party is desirable but a crush at a dinner party is a disaster both for those seated and those trying to serve. If the numbers do not fit then change the venue or shed a few guests.

courtesy of Searcy's

If catering at home, one simple luxury which could transform your evening is to pay for one pair of extra hands, even if they only wash up. Do not rely on friends who say they will help and then forget. With no help at all remember you will miss out on all the gossip until the meal is over.

At the very start of the planning, think hard about your guests. Unless you enjoy a confrontational evening consider the mix of people. If one of your dearest friends is likely to annoy or irritate everyone else then try to make a point of only inviting them to cocktail parties.

The next hurdle for an at-home event is choosing the food. It used to be simple when hardly anyone had allergies and people were too polite to object to what was placed in front of them. Try to remember any religious eating restrictions, stories about food-poisoning or allergies. If it is a no-choice meal then avoid all shellfish, scallops etc and nuts to minimise the risk. Better still, ask them outright as this will avoid those famous words "Oh, did I forget to mention that . . . " which sends a chill down every host's spine. This may all have started to sound more like an assault course than a pleasure but advance planning will avoid many problems that can occur on the day.

courtesy of Searcy's

When planning your menu be realistic - all the glossy pictures in the cookery books are like the supermodels: lovely to look at, but

courtesy of Searcy's & Joanna Plumbe Photography

impossible for most of us to imitate without looking a complete fool. If you have by now been frightened off the party at home, start thinking about your local restaurants. Whenever possible, choose somewhere you have been and can trust. If you wish to talk the event through with a member of staff do telephone before turning up, to ensure that a knowledgeable person is available. Very few places have a senior member of staff "spare" just in case someone turns up to talk to them. If you are not expected they may not be able to help at that moment and you may leave feeling quite unwanted.

Having chosen the venue, ensure that you do not try to get them to serve a meal that is different from their normal menu. Also, believe their estimate on numbers - no walls are elastic. Another vital point to consider is whether you are happy with the atmosphere of the venue. If you want to let your hair down then choose a relaxed establishment, but if you want a quiet and dignified party then make sure you will not be somewhere that encourages the exact opposite.

After all this, choose a realistic time that everyone can make, check they accept your type of credit card - embarrassing to have to finish the night in a police cell - and finally if I have not frightened everyone into dining alone for the rest of your days - enjoy your parties!

Helen Stevenson, Farlam Hall

Canapé is not a word I like - it sounds somehow wet and feeble. What could be further from the truth? These little beauties, if prepared and served with style, can be absolute winners, providing food and indeed entertainment at excellent value. They also give the host some control on the timetable.

Canapés

Having run one of London's most prestigious catering companies for the past 20 years, I have realised what an important role canapés play in the party scene. Much of our time is spent developing new ideas for the most outrageous and spectacular presentation and design. However, to produce canapés of this standard in your own home would be incredibly time-consuming and frankly, a nightmare! My theory is that if you are having a party at home, you should either employ caterers to produce something wild and witty or you should make something very simple, but of the best quality, and present it with style.

- Cut the ripest fig in half and roll a piece of prosciutto on top of it.

- Fill a bowl with crisp radishes and cooked tiny Jersey new potatoes and serve them with aïoli.

- Make bruschetta from loaves of ciabatta. Toast slices until crisp in the oven, then spread with pesto or tapenade, roasted artichokes, sun dried tomatoes and crumbled feta cheese. You can buy all of these ingredients from a good supermarket.

- Skewer 3" pieces of salmon or chicken breast on wooden skewers and marinate with soy, ginger and lemon grass for a taste of Thai, or with fresh herbs, virgin olive oil, chillies and garlic for a hint of Provence, or cajun spices for Creole. Marinate for at least 12 hours, then cook quickly in a hot oven and serve with a dipping sauce.

- Buy a side of smoked salmon and carve into thickish slices and encourage guests to make their own canapés by offering them slices of fresh soda bread, warmed blinis or toasted muffins with a pot of crème fraîche.

- Roast almonds with virgin olive oil, sea salt and serve with delicious olives.

- Create Tuscan olives by buying the cheapest tinned black olives (with stones), drain and cover with olive oil, a couple of hot dried chillies, two cloves of garlic and a sprig of thyme.

- Make your own crisp fried vegetable chips by deep frying thin slices of beetroot, sweet potato, parsnip, plantain and celeriac.

Some of our canapés that could be produced at home include Caesar salad tarts, puy lentils and chorizo bruschetta, wild mushroom tarts with lemon hollandaise, little pots of curry sauce with either chicken, salmon or prawns to dip in, mini burgers which we serve in tiny seeded buns with tomato relish, mini fish and chips (we use either brill or cod) in cones of the FT, seared mini steaks with a leaf of rocket and parmesan mayonnaise on a toasted soda croute, red onion marmalade tarts, strawberries dipped in dark and white chocolate . . . I could go on forever!

Be inspired when you think about presenting your canapés. Think of the time of year and what elements you could incorporate, be it rose hips and old man's beard in autumn, witches' broomsticks and masks for Halloween or frosted fruits, gilded vegetables and

courtesy of Searcy's

angel hair for Christmas. Buy unusual plates when you see them, particularly when you are in Spain, Portugal or Italy on holiday. And always buy ingredients of the best quality. Fill glasses with green apples, lemons, mushrooms or roses and put your plate of canapés on top.

Be adventurous and fill your garden pots with woodland mosses, acorns, chestnuts and fungi. With a glass plate on top, none of the bugs will climb into your food! Use terracotta flower pots, children's nursery chairs, beautiful cushions or hat boxes.

courtesy of The Ice Box

Don't think you can make up canapés a long time in advance - they do tend to go soggy if they sit around. You can do the preparation in advance but put them together as near to your guests' arrival as possible. In particular, don't fill tarts too long in advance. Bruschetta, on the other hand, improves by being a bit soggy so that all the pesto/tapenade soaks into the base.

Amuse your guests with your presentation. Much of the pleasure of eating has to do with eye appeal and if you can make your guests have a chuckle as well as loving your delicious bits to eat, you have achieved a success.

Janie Lloyd-Owen, by word of mouth

Porter: Drink, sir, is a great provoker of three things.
Macduff: What three things does drink especially provoke?
Porter: Marry, sir, nose-painting, sleep, and urine.
Lechery, sir, it provokes; it provokes the desire, but it takes away the performance.

Shakespeare, Macbeth.

Having found yourself a caterer that seems to speak your language then the next step is to decide on your menu. Any caterer worth their salt (ho ho ho) will provide you with a selection of menus and will advise you from the outset the various implications when hearing your initial ideas. Planning good parties is often about being practical. I was desperate to get involved with the planning of our wedding, along with my wife. Big mistake - huge! I found that my ideas were overelaborate and impractical. My mother in law is overwhelmingly practical and in the end it avoided huge rows just to let them get on with it.

The type of catering will depend on a number of factors - the location, the time of year, the number of guests and the amount of hard earned cash at your disposal.

Buffets or sit down meals?

HOT OR COLD?

The type of party you have may be governed by many factors - space, time of year, budget, equipment available, style and of course food required. Once some of these decisions have been made you have to think: do I want a sit down served meal, sit down buffet or stand up buffet and hot or cold food or a mixture?

A buffet was originally a piece of furniture - a sideboard - from which food was served, but today it is recognised as a party where the food is displayed on a large table and either the guests come up and serve themselves or they are served an array of culinary delights by staff.

The advantage of a buffet over a sit down meal is essentially that the event is more informal and guests mingle and chat. Even if they sit down with their friends they are almost certain to meet other guests when queuing for the buffet table. Also, as we all initially eat with our eyes, the food can appear more spectacular when spread out on a table in a colourful and appetising manner.

Normally buffets are 2 course meals, main course and sweets, but variations are the addition of a canapé course when first arriving at the party or solely a canapé reception. Buffets can be hot or cold or a mixture of both, and if hot the food can be displayed on hot plates (those with halogen lights are particularly useful as they not only warm the food from above and below but also throw light on the display, making it look more appetising). Chafing dishes can keep food hot for a long period of time without drying out.

A hot buffet can consist of a variety of casseroles, lasagnas or moussakas served with new potatoes, dauphinois potatoes or boulangère potatoes together with a selection of vegetables or salads. A carvery can also be an impressive sight with large joints of ham, lamb, beef or pork sliced for each guest as they reach the buffet table whilst the ultimate alfresco buffet is a spectacular barbecue.

A cold buffet table can look absolutely stunning if planned to combine an array of colour, textures and heights. Large cascades of fruit can add a touch of elegance and opulence and lobsters and large prawns can be used as decorations as well as to eat.

A formal sit down meal was the norm for many years but the buffet is now equally popular. The advantages of the formal meal are that everyone sits down, usually but not always to a seating plan, to a 2 ,3, 4 or 5 course hot or cold meal that is served. Accordingly it is popular with people who wish to sit and talk to their friends, and also with the elderly (and some of those younger) who are grateful for not having to stand for several hours as often happens at a buffet. The major operational problem for the

caterer here is that the venue must have appropriate facilities - cookers, hot cupboards, water heaters or at the very least sufficiently strong electrical power to enable portable equipment to be used. There have been many near misses when the electricity has blown at critical moments!

courtesy of Irvin Leisure & Joanna Plumbe Photography

At the end of the day the choice of style of meal often depends as much on practicalities (e.g. area and facilities available) as on the host's personal choice. Either can be excellent and new variations are always appearing as people strive to be slightly different. I have noticed recently that omelette parties have started to be popular, either as a brunch or for a late night party.

A tip when having a finger or fork buffet: a clip attached to the plate is a great help. It is difficult to eat when one hand is holding the plate and the other the glass!

Whatever you choose I hope you have a good time.

Linda Baker, Linda's Pantry

While some hosts and hostesses enjoy themselves and have a great time at their own parties, there are others who find the whole thing quite a chore. In order to make a party something to remember even the most reluctant host can turn on the style. What about asking your local Indian restaurant for a special price for catering in your own home?

Cold meats can also be absolutely marvellous, many butchers now provide food that is beautifully presented - book in advance you might be surprised. Here are a few tips to consider when entertaining at home.

Entertaining at home

Many of the tried and tested techniques employed in successful outside catering can be adapted to ensure the smooth running of a memorable party at home.

The most important piece of advice is to plan thoroughly. While you should appear to be totally relaxed on the day, everything should have been highly organised. Sit with a list and plan everything down to the last teaspoon.

Walk the course as professionals do when managing a party . Check out every detail from where guests are going to park their cars to how they will find their coats at the end of the evening.

When your guests arrive, look as though you're enjoying yourself. Appear fresh and relaxed. Throwing money at a party doesn't make it a good one - you've got to enjoy it.

A lot of people feel apprehensive walking in to a party. Make sure that they are given a drink as soon as possible and that they are looked after. If someone wanders off outside, ask a helper to take them out a glass or some canapés.

Employing an extra pair of hands takes some of the responsibility away from the host. Many people make themselves far too much work when entertaining at home. Keep your dinner parties at home quite simple - for example, these days there's no need to offer a huge choice of puddings; nicely prepared exotic fresh fruit is a welcome change.

A special occasion can always be made more memorable by hiring a small marquee. Lighting is very important, with spots on tables and lots and lots of candles. Flowers can transform a room and coloured linen can have a magical effect.

A final tip to party organisers is: if there are going to be a reasonable number of guests and some music, do let the local police know what is going on. They really do appreciate it.

Sam Chalmers, Chimneys Outside Catering Company and Chimneys Restaurant

courtesy of The Carnegie Club at Skibo Castle

110

It is often said that first impressions count the most. If you manage to make your table look magnificent - or just different but organised - you will have hit the ground running and that's half the battle.

Setting the perfect dinner table

The Skibo dining room is set today as it was 100 years ago when Andrew Carnegie hosted his first family dinner before he went on to invite the Rockefellers, Rudyard Kipling and the nobility of his time. Then, as today, the main dining room table would comfortably seat 22 people with 10 each side and one at each end. The huge oak carved leather chairs packed tightly with their straw cushions surround the table as if somehow guarding the perfectly laid silver and glassware.

In order to set this mighty table it is important to follow a certain order. When laying the table it is first important to know how many people you are seating in order to correctly space out the chairs and place mats. The mats once clean are laid two finger widths in from the table's edge so that when the large main plates are served the plate does not have its rim overlapping the table, inviting an accident. The cutlery is then placed in reverse order ie. sweet first and starter last, working out from the place mat. Cutlery is laid at right angles to the table's edge, each piece parallel to the next. It is imperative that once the silverware is polished it does not come into contact with human hands again until your guests sit down. We therefore suggest that white gloves be worn (preferably serving gloves - as opposed to ski or boxing, that is!) or a clean napkin used in placing the cutlery so that finger marks are avoided.

The dessert fork is placed to the left, closest to the place mat with the dessert spoon on the right. The main cutlery follows with the steak knife on the right, blade in, and the steak fork on the left. The fish knife, follows the steak knife as the fish fork follows the steak fork. Starter fork and knife are the last down unless, as in some houses, the bread or side knife is placed furthest out on the right hand side. If not, it is then placed on the side plate, blade out, right centre of the plate, which will be found between each table setting.

At Skibo wine is served in 30oz glasses. These are placed 6" above the steak knife in a triangle—white bottom, red right and water left. Glasses should be highly polished to a squeak, washed by hand using hot soapy water and polished using the steam from boiling water with a tablespoon of spirit vinegar added.

Cruets should of course be full and always remember salt three, pepper six... holes that is. For certain meals a black pepper grinder will be required, making the cruet duet a trio!

Butter dishes join the dinner setting next to the cruet family just before dinner is served. Crushed ice is a useful addition to keep butter firm, but always remember the strange correlation "the harder the butter, the softer the bread".

For floral arrangements and candles, always work from the centre out decreasing in size as you go. Not so obtrusive that your guests need a hedge-trimmer to improve communication. Try to use flowers to complement the season. Scottish heather is a castle favourite when in bloom.

In order to check your work, stand at the end of the table and stare down the line - all should be in place, not an inch too high or too low.

As for the table plan, our Head Butler James Allen's advice is "never think too hard or you will find yourself lumbered with several versions of the same plan". My advice? "Always sit yourself between the interesting and the beautiful!"

Finally, your dinner should not be just a meal, more an experience shared, an evening together, where conversation is swapped and friendships bonded.

Richard Hallam, Operations Manager, Carnegie Club at Skibo Castle

First impressions are often the ones that count. I fondly recall a mother at our children's school strolling off into the local wood. On inquiring as to her well being with some concern, she waved a set of secateurs. As I drove off, I glanced in my rear-view mirror and saw her emerging triumphant from the woods with her arms full of holly.

Say it with flowers

Choosing and using flowers when planning a party is no mean task. They can be used in the simplest way, such as a bunch picked from the garden and put in an old cracked jug in the middle of the table. They can be arranged in the priceless silver bowl you inherited from your grandmother. You can use them to create a theme. Or you could spend a fortune, have flowers everywhere and all your guests will think that you have won the lottery.

Listed below are some guidelines which should stand you in good stead when organising a party.

Rule One: Unless you have all the time in the world, why not avoid the stress and the chipped nails and having to wash your hands in bleach to get them clean and . . . employ a florist!

Rule Two: Table centres:- First and foremost, do remember that your guests have come to see you so don't make the arrangements too big. Of course, sometimes you have to have one of those parties to pay back the people you owe but don't really want to have and you know the conversation will be sticky. In those cases, make the flower arrangement as big and as dramatic as you like! At least it will get the conversation going and when you've had enough you can hide behind it!

Rule Three: For a small party:- Unless your house desperately needs redecorating, don't overdo the use of flowers. Flowers should enhance your house. One vase in the sitting room with plenty of greenery and flowers to complement your colour scheme on a table that is not too covered in ornaments and photographs is more than enough, with maybe a small posy on a coffee or side table.

Rule Four: For a larger party in the home:- You may want to do more for a large party. The entrance hall is a good place to have an arrangement of flowers. It is welcoming to your guests and if one of your guests comments on them it can be a good morale boost for the nervous hostess.

Rule Five: Smell:- The fact that you have burnt the Melba toast, over-grilled the crème brulée, or the dog has just messed under the table can be masked by flowers that have a wonderful scent. Lilies of some variety, Freesia, Sweet Peas, Lily of the Valley, Jasmine - the list is quite long - try to include some of these in your flowers. Don't go overboard though or you will have hay fever sufferers sneezing over your first course.

Rule Six: When doing the flowers yourself, always remember that anything you pick from the garden, hedgerows or fields will need a good drink in fresh water (at least two hours) before arranging it. This will allow any dodgy ones time to wilt so they can go in the bin rather than onto your dining table where you will have to drag them out all over your beautifully laid table at the last minute.

Rule Seven: Buying from the local florist prior to doing the flowers yourself. Make sure the flowers are fresh and they haven't been sitting in the shop for a week. If you know your florist well and he or she does not mind that you are having this wonderful party and haven't commissioned them to do the flowers, ask if they are fresh. Otherwise look carefully at the leaves on the flowers. If they have all been removed, or are yellowing at all, or the stems are limp - don't buy them. They might well be dead before the evening is out. You can guarantee that the guest you were most nervous about will be heard commenting as they walk down your front path: "Lovely evening, pity about the flowers!"

Rule Eight: The best way to buy from the local florist is to work out what you want to use and in what quantities and order them. Most florists will go to a flower market on Monday and Thursday. Some also have a lorry from Holland, known as 'The Dutchman', who comes to call on them during the week, though not always on a set day. If you need flowers for Monday, Tuesday or Wednesday, order them the previous Thursday. Equally, if you need flowers for Thursday, Friday, Saturday or

Sunday, order them the previous Monday. If you dare, tell your florist the date of the party and that you will need the flowers perfect for that day. Some flowers arrive in tight bud and need a few days to come out. I am sure your florist will oblige, lest you take your future business elsewhere.

Rule Nine: If you really want to go over the top, don't do it in half measures. Go for the whole works: archways of flowers, flowers garlanding down the bannisters, flowers tied with ribbons to the backs of chairs, flowers and fruit down the full length of the dining table, an entire garden planted in the centre of your conservatory table, trees and flowering shrubs brought into your sitting/drawing room. This is when you really seriously need a florist who can design an entire theme throughout your house and a marquee - go for it!

Rule Ten: Remember, it will always cost more than you thought it would, unless they come out of your garden. Flowers for any form of entertainment are in a different league from the bunches of flowers sold off cheaply on a Friday evening in your local supermarket. Unfortunately!

THERE ARE ALSO SOME DANGERS!

Water can do untold damage to furniture. One of the authors of this article is fortunately married to an antique furniture restorer so on the odd occasion when water has inadvertently got where it should not have, rescue has been at hand.

Arrangements placed in effective but precarious places have a nasty habit of falling off messily and noisily and usually at just the wrong moment. Make certain they are securely fixed with 'oasis fix' or that they are wired to something. Mantelpieces are a major danger zone, especially those high up above big, hot, open fires. The oasis in the flower arrangement can dry out very quickly, which alters the weight of the arrangement dramatically. Flower arrangements falling eight or nine feet make quite a mess and dried or drying flowers burn quite well!

Pedestal arrangements near dance floors in a marquee are a positive no-no. They will either be picked up and taken to dance by an over-zealous and more often than not over-refreshed male admirer, or knocked over by a rather unsteady passer-by resulting very possibly in a broken limb or a previously perfect bosom being punctured by a rose thorn.

Finally, arranging flowers is exhausting work. So, if your florist is also your friend, don't be too upset when he or she slumps down under one of their sensational creations and starts snoring gently.

Caro Dickinson & Harriet Warde-Aldam, Flowers Unlimited

courtesy of Flowers Unlimited

If people make parties and they often do, it's important to remember that people are only as good as their host or hostess is at introducing them. Important as an introduction is though, there is more to it than that.

Perfect manners

So I want to make a party perfect. Fine. Polish the cutlery, wipe the mats, brush the chairs, trim the candles, polish the plates. Does this make a good party? Oh yes, but this is a long way from what makes a really good party. Real success lies in matters far more philosophical and esoteric.

The guests have finished dinner, some are standing in the hall, others are reclining in the armchairs. Everyone is lulled by good food and wine. Now, and only now, does the real work begin.

Someone wants a whisky. Do they know whisky well? I ask. No, so I bring them three. I tell them that the first is light and soft, the second is well balanced between light and peaty and the third is truly the whisky of great mountains, storms and wild places (Lagavullin, of course). This is the first clue to what makes a really great party - always go the extra mile!

Someone wants a cognac. This marks a beginning. Every time I pass him I will steal a subtle glance at his glass. Just as he drains it I will be standing there with a fresh glass. This goes on for as long as necessary, but every glass I bring will be the first and, if necessary, I will repeatedly reassure the guest of this. How do I define failure? Simple - someone has to ask for something. So, the second clue to a truly great party - anticipate!

After a while the real work begins. Everyone is enjoying their first drink for the sixth or seventh time and the evening is turning very cosy. Everyone is also aware of a subtle and unspoken code of practice between me and them. They know that I will remember them as perfect ladies and perfect gentlemen, no matter what!

My deeds are not yet done, however. In the morning, as our guests come down to breakfast, I will reassure everyone that I have absolutely no recollection whatsoever of anything that took place the previous evening.

So the third and most important ingredient of a truly outstanding party - be discreet! Just now and then, however, a guest insists on telling me how bad they feel. Despite my selective memory loss they persist. How can I resolve this? I cannot allow myself to admit that anyone took alcohol because it is against my professional ethics. I have to find a way to maintain my dignity and theirs. In these cases I usually fall back on my standard phrase; "Ah, but Sir, do remember that notoriety is sometimes better than obscurity". Laughter follows and all is well again.

James Allen, Head Butler, Skibo Castle

courtesy of Skibo Castle

114

Lighting your home can be both functional and decorative. In the great scheme of things, however, it is seldom used to the best effect - this is a pity because unusual lighting both inside and outside your house can really make an impact. Obvious choices such as log fires and candles can make a great difference to the atmosphere of a room, but there are numerous other options. Here are a few.

Lighting in the home

Home lighting has undergone considerable change over the last ten years. Hitherto the lighting fixtures in your house were predominantly centre ceiling, cord hanging lanterns of purpose. 'Bring on the night, sweep in the dark . . .' it no longer mattered, modern man switched on his electric lamp and, with a single bulb, bathed his dwelling in a bright glow allowing him to continue the day's activities in the face of tradition and nature. In time sophistication crept in - instead of the generalised 'space' illumination, the householder harked back to the nostalgic, cosy candle glow and remembered that a soft, more localised light source next to a chair, on a side table, would offer a warmer, more cosy ambience than the utilitarian suspended fitting. Table lamps, shades, smaller bulbs . . . there emerged a choice, a potential for alteration and adjustment to personal taste.

Today you'll find a host of different domestic light fittings available - all different in specification, brightness, beam angle, appearance and size. 'Low Voltage' lights, miniature bulbs, dichroic lighting and especially domestic dimming facilities: all these new 'tools' have allowed much greater options as to where light sources may be installed and how the fittings themselves may be created. Where before light was automatically a single ceiling fitting, today multiple light sources allow a distinct choice between function and 'mood' lighting.

So how does this affect the potential 'at home' entertainer? Obviously a host/hostess would prefer to have the house illuminated so that fine features are emphasised, guests feel welcome and any imperfections are hidden away - and that's before any concerns about special effects.

Here are a few helpful hints:

- Turn off the central, single fitting. You are not about to start hoovering so you don't need your social rooms lit up like a football pitch. Dimming down is a possibility but only if the fitting is an interesting feature in itself, a chandelier for example—something not found in most living rooms perhaps. Track lighting, being more specific in its task than the traditional bulb, can be dimmed for a more gentle effect.

- Low-level bulbs offer the 'cosy option'. Like using candles - an old-fashioned but still popular method—low-level table lamps will offer a gentle, soft light output in a localised area. Part of the process of creating a cosy atmosphere is to keep away from lighting the whole space, but instead to create 'gaps' between illuminated points in the room. This way the room develops focus points which, in turn, suggests intimacy.

- Uplights - easy to install as they need no fixing, just a socket to plug into. Useful for two main purposes: firstly they can be feature lighting - placed in front of, beneath, or indeed behind a plant, fireplace or similar architectural feature to enhance the object; secondly, simply placed along a featureless wall they will send a pillar of light upwards thus creating a feature, where before there was none. One could also have these uplights coloured for a more festive feel.

- Projected patterns: try a bit of 'art light'. If you are bored with white walls and ceilings it is possible to acquire lamps which, when fitted with a metal disc, can project patterns - perhaps even names and ages for a personal touch. Don't be embarrassed that you've reached 30, 40 or 50 - splash it all over the ceiling in a primary colour! This is a useful tool for theming a party: a leaf pattern in green and gold suggesting woodlands, clouds for a sky, a cartoon witch on a broom-stick for Halloween - there are a wide range of options before even considering custom-made examples.

Fisher

Lighting is terribly important, but catering is absolutely fundamental to all occasions. If you are looking for outside assistance there are a number of rules to follow.

Finding a good catering company

By far the best way to find a caterer is by word of mouth. If you have experienced good food and service at a friend's party, ask them who they employed. If your neighbours' daughter was married last month and they were happy with their caterers you could not have a better recommendation.

You need to decide what kind of caterer you want. Clearly the requirements for a child's birthday party differ from those of a large wedding. If you contact a company from an advertisement in Tatler or the Yellow Pages, spend time discussing your party with them and ask to see sample menus. You will be able to tell a lot about the company from their menus and their presentation. Meet someone from the company as it is important to get on with the person who is going to create your party and play a big part on the day. Ask for references. A good catering company will be happy to supply testimonial letters from satisfied clients. Ask friends and neighbours if they have heard any comments on the companies you are considering.

Get quotes and sample menus from at least two catering companies. Sample their food. Choose some dishes from their sample menus and try them out. You will be charged for this, but it will help you make your decision. Do they taste good? What is the presentation like?

Get a clear breakdown of what is included in the 'per-head' price as this does vary considerably.

When you have considered the menus and the costs, the decision frequently rests on how you feel about the representative. Do you feel they value your custom? Do you feel your party will be important to them?

Kaye Thompson, The Creative Catering Company

courtesy of Searcy's & Joanna Plumbe Photography

Equipment for small parties

Unless you happen to have been lucky enough to inherit china and glass passed down from six generations of forbears (and even if you have, chances are it is all far too precious to use anyway!), you will need to use a hire company to obtain your china, cutlery and glass, not to mention tables and chairs. Of course everybody's taste is different, but if you are not an experienced party-giver our tip is to keep things simple. Simple yet elegant china, glass and cutlery will never look out of place.

A typical list of items available for hire might include:

China: Plates (all sizes), soup and dessert bowls, coffee and tea cups, casserole dishes, vegetable and pasta dishes, salad bowls, coffee and tea pots, sugar bowls and cream jugs

Glassware: Salad bowls of various sizes, serving platters in different shapes, sizes and colours, jugs, cake plates and cheeseboards

Cutlery: Stainless steel or silver plate, including serving pieces such as cheese and butter knives, fish knives and forks, cake slices, etc. Also candelabra and candlesticks, wedding cake stands and serving dishes

Glasses: Glasses for every type of drink and occasion

Tables: Rectangular and round tables with seating capacities from four to twelve

Chairs: Simple pine folding chairs, gilt or coloured banqueting chairs with padded seats

Linen: Damask table cloths and napkins in a range of colours, shapes and sizes, as well as service cloths and tea towels

Bar equipment: Jugs, ice bins, and serving trays

Cooking: Chafing dishes, turbo ovens, gas boiling rings, fridges/freezers

Equipment: Microwaves, hot plates, hot cupboards, hot water urns, coffee percolators, and soup tureens. Not to mention cake tins, roasting trays, saucepans of enormous capacity

When choosing an equipment hire company, ask for their colour brochure and price list and do a bit of comparative shopping. Most prices will be quoted ex-VAT, and there are likely to be delivery charges. Make sure you check their terms and conditions as well as deposit requirements, cancellation policies and breakage charges. If you are hiring equipment in a non-peak time (i.e. not Christmas or mid-summer) companies may be more willing to negotiate special arrangements (like length of hire) so it is always worth asking. Most companies will take back if dirty, and charge you a percentage of the hire charge to cover the cost of washing it. This is particularly useful for large parties, but even a dinner party for 14 involving four courses can create quite a mountain of washing-up.

If you don't wish to rely on photographs in a brochure, then go and have a look at what types of equipment they have in stock. Don't be afraid to ask advice about the quantities and types of equipment you need. These people are professionals and will be only too happy to be of assistance.

Amanda Stephenson, Gorgeous Gourmets

Parties under canvas

Parties under canvas, if organised correctly, are great fun and have many advantages. The host is able to hold a much larger, more intimate party at a venue of their choice, whilst reducing the risk of any damage to the surrounding area which might be caused by a large influx of guests. Marquees and structures can be themed for an event by the use of coloured fabrics, props, lighting, and other accessories—anything is possible at a cost. In fact, cost is probably the only major disadvantage of organising a party under canvas, as generally it will be more expensive than the equivalent in a hall or hotel.

Once you have weighed up the acquired atmosphere and the outdoor party experience against the costs involved and have decided that a marquee is what your party needs, you need to find a marquee contractor.

The best source would be through personal recommendation. Failing this, most suppliers advertise in telephone publications, event guides, and magazines. It is very important to find a reputable contractor. The majority belong to the Made Up Textiles Association (MUTA) the trade body for marquee contractors, which operates a very strict code of practice (List of members available from MUTA 01827 - 52337).

On finding a suitable contractor always insist on a full site visit and survey, these will be free of charge and will provide you with valuable information and adventurous ideas on what is available and what is possible. There are two main types of tents: traditional marquees and framed pavilions. A traditional marquee has centre supporting poles and guy ropes around the perimeter and the roof and walls are generally made from white canvas (although PVC fabrics are also becoming popular). A framed pavilion is generally an aluminium portal frame with a PVC covering which has no centre poles or exterior stakes and ropes. As a result they are easier to fit alongside buildings and in restricted places. Aluminium framed pavilions are generally more stable in adverse weather conditions, they tend to take slightly longer to erect and dismantle, and are more expensive to hire than their traditional counterparts. Personal preference, visual attractiveness, limitations of site and cost will determine the type of structure most suitable, and again advice should be sought from the contractor during the site survey. It is very important during the site survey that the contractor be made aware of any underground or overhead services i.e. drains, gas pipes, electricity cables, etc.

The organiser of the event should ensure that the current power supply is capable of expanding to meet the requirements of the marquee. If there is any doubt, consult a qualified electrical contractor.

Checklist of things to do:

- Confirm number of guests
- Confirm delivery/completion and dismantle dates
- Confirm furniture type and quantity (allow for catering)
- Agree internal layout of marquee
- Agree colours and style of interior decoration
- Confirm payment terms (deposit required etc)
- Be sure your contractor is aware of the position of underground services
- Ensure your power supply is adequate, if in doubt consult a qualified electrical contractor
- Consider fire precautions, provide for extinguishers
- Keep all flaps and doors closed in windy conditions
- Consult your contractor who is qualified to advise on safety in your marquee
- Inform the contractor if you need the marquee in place prior to the eve of the event
- Stagger the arrival of various contractors, eg Caterers are unable to set up before the roof lining is in place
- Beware of confusion between metric and imperial measurements
- Update your contractor(s) with any changes to guest numbers, date, etc prior to the event

All of the above points are very important. You will find that your contractor will be very helpful in supplying you with the knowledge and understanding to have a very organised, safe and enjoyable party under canvas.

Danco Plc

The cigar – the art of tasting

The appreciation of fine cigars, like the appreciation of fine wines, is an exceptional art. Here are a few guidelines from the world's most respected connoisseur of cigars: Zino Davidoff.

THE FINE CIGAR

A fine cigar is handmade using only 100% tobacco (machine rolled cigars with a binder and/or wrapper of homogenised tobacco are generally not worth smoking).

The most superior cigar in the world is one that you enjoy at a distinguished moment, allowing you to relax and savour that which gives you the utmost enjoyment . . . The most superior cigar in the world is invaluable!

ETIQUETTE

Enjoying a cigar is a sophisticated pastime. The true connoisseur is refined. He enjoys his cigars without disturbing the people in his surrounding environment.

ATTITUDE

The cigar connoisseur does not "smoke", he savours . . . because every draw should be an experience of succulent pleasure to the palate.

THE ART OF CIGAR SELECTION

The connoisseur selects the cigar that coincides with the moment; the cigar that permits him to relax and awards him the most pleasure. Price is not a factor for the experienced aficionado, his choice is based upon both personal preference and on available time, so he can cherish all the qualities of the cigar at his leisure.

The following list provides some useful guidelines:

• Senoritas	The short break
• Panatellas	The day's first cigar
• Petit Coronas	Before dinner
• Coronas	Extending a luxurious lunch
• Grand Coronas	An hour of leisure
• Double Coronas	Crowning a regal dinner
• Giant Double Coronas	For the exceptional moment

THE BAND

Cigar smokers often wonder whether or not to remove the cigar band. Zino advises against this. Since cigar bands are manually put onto most hand-made cigars, there is always the chance that these bands will stick to the wrapper and damage it while being removed. Therefore it is highly recommended to leave the band on for at least the first third of the cigar.

CUTTING

How the sealed end of the cigar is cut ultimately determines the quality of the draw, the subtlety and intensity of the cigar's aroma, in addition to assuring that the cigar remains evenly lit.

The cut should be directly proportional to the thickness of the cigar. For example, you would not make the same cut for a Davidoff Grand Cru No 3, as you would for an Ambassadrice. Whatever method you choose to make the cut, it should be clean and large enough to permit a proper draw.

The ultimate cigar cutting instruments are the Davidoff scissors and the double edged "Zino" cutter, which have been specifically designed for achieving a properly cut cigar. They yield a clear and neat circular cut, regardless of the cigar's diameter.

FINDING THE RIGHT CIGAR

- Sample cigars of the same size from different brands - say a 5$\frac{1}{2}$ or 5" corona or Mareva - to find the blend you like.

- If you smoke more than one cigar per day, remember subsequent ones should have equal or fuller flavour. Never follow a full cigar with a lighter one.

- Slow burning, heavy gauge cigars offer a bigger flavour than slender ones of the same marque.

- It is a popular misconception that dark cigars are fuller flavoured. Not so. If anything, dark wrappers add sweetness, while light ones add a touch of dryness to the taste.

HOW TO HANDLE YOUR CIGAR

- Cigars should be stored at between 16° and 18°, with humidity at around 72% for Dominican cigars.

- Before lighting, hold the cigar between index finger and thumb and squeeze it gently. If in prime condition, it should feel firm but springy. The wrapper leaf should have a sheen of natural oils.

- To prepare, use a guillotine or cutter to lop off most of the cap. Be sure to leave part intact to prevent the wrapper unravelling.

- Lighting a cigar is an important business. Never rush. Char the open end in flame to prepare it for ignition. Then place it between the lips and draw while rotating it.

- When smoking, do not inhale, but gently draw the smoke into your mouth and roll it around your taste buds. Treat it like fine malt whisky!

- Two points of etiquette: first, don't flick the ash off, but let it fall in its own time - preferably into an ash tray! Second, never stub out a cigar. Let it go out in its own time.

Remember Zino Davidoff's legendary motto "Smoke less but smoke the best"

Davidoff Distribution UK Ltd

It was Kipling that said "And a woman is only a woman, but a good cigar is a Smoke". What a saucy boy. Well, far be it from me to comment but certainly both have contributed much to ensure an excellent evening!

courtesy of Stapleford Park

Professional associations

BALLOONS

The National Association of Balloon Artists and Suppliers (NABAS) is an independent association of balloon companies of all sizes in the UK. They have members throughout the country and maintain a database at their HQ which is manned during normal working hours by a full time assistant. They will be delighted to offer advice and supply details of NABAS members local to your event. Member companies comply with industry standard practice and carry out their work to an industry standard. The association is managed by an executive committee of elected officials from within the industry and they have specialist advisers on matters such as pyrotechnics, balloon releases and the environment. The association employs a full time secretariat to assist it in maintaining contact with members and keeping them up to date with the latest information in the industry.

courtesy of Party Pieces

NABAS - The Balloon Association
Katepwa House, Ashfield Park Avenue, Ross-on-Wye, Herefordshire HR9 5AX
Tel: 01989 762 204 Contact: Allison Tolley

CORPORATE HOSPITALITY AND EVENTS

The Corporate Hospitality and Event Association has now been in existence for 10 years and is the only professional organisation truly representing companies involved in the Hospitality and Event Industry. Potential members are fully vetted before being allowed to join the Association and particular attention is paid to their trading record with references required from both clients and trade related companies who have had dealings with the applicant.

Corporate Hospitality and Event Association ltd
Arena House, 66-68 Pentonville Road, Islington, London N1 9HS
Tel.: 0171 278 0288

COSTUMES

The British Costume Association was originally established over twelve years ago as the British Fancy Dress and Allied Trades Association by a group of wholesalers and retailers looking to establish good trading practice and a forum for discussion on issues arising within the business. Nowadays our scope has broadened and aside from our costume manufacturers, hirers and retailers we also have members involved in costume-related promotion and PR activities, theatrical work, film, TV work and prop hire.

The British Costume Association
Peter Rigby (Membership & General Secretary)
c/o Antrix, 8 Waldron Drive, Loose, Maidstone, Kent ME15 9TG
Tel.: 01622 744 711

ELECTRICAL INSTALLATIONS

National Inspection Council for Electrical Installation Contractors (NICEIC)
Contractors on the NICEIC roll are required to carry out their work with materials of good quality, installed by competent electricians, adequately and appropriately supervised. All electrical work carried out by NICEIC approved contractors must conform to the current edition of the Requirements for Electrical Installations (BS

courtesy of Irvin Leisure & Joanna Plumbe Photography

7671:1992), published by the Institution of Electrical Engineers, and all other relevant Codes of Practice and Guidance Documents. After a full and detailed inspection, contractors approved by the NICEIC sign an undertaking to work to these standards and are regularly reinspected by members of the 40 strong field force of Inspecting Engineers to ensure that they continue to do so. Those whose work consistently falls below the required standards are removed from the roll.

Through its complaints procedure, the NICEIC investigates all allegations that approved contractors have not complied with the Council's technical standard and, where substantiated, requires the contractor to correct any faults at no extra cost to the consumer. If the contractor is unwilling to do so then, under the guarantee of standards scheme, the NICEIC will appoint another contractor to correct the deviations, again at no additional cost to the specifier or consumer.

National Inspection Council for Electrical Installation Contracting
Vintage House, 37 Albert Embankment, London SE1 7UJ.
Tel.: 0171 564 2323

FACE PAINTING

The Face Painting Association (FACE) was set up to promote a high standard of design and artistic ability as well as an awareness of hygiene and safety in face painting. All our members are covered by our group public liability insurance. The membership is drawn from all areas of the British Isles and regardless of experience all members have to pass an assessment before they may join. We boast several authors on face painting and also several teachers of this skill. Many of the members hold an advanced certificate in face painting and are experienced body painters.

courtesy of Masquerade

FACE The Face Painting Association
c/o 63 Crown Road, Barkingside, Ilford, Essex IG6 1NN
Tel.: 07000 FACE PAINT (07000 3223 72468)

MARQUEES

Made-Up Textiles Association (MUTA)
MUTA is the recognised trade association policing safety standards for marquees. Members must meet specified criteria to be certified, and spot checks are regularly carried out to ensure that they are using flame-retardant materials and that tents are erected to the Code of Practice.

Made-Up Textiles Association
42 Heath Street, Tamworth, Staffordshire B79 7JH
Tel.: 01827 52337

OUTDOOR EVENTS

National Outdoor Events Association
NOEA is the specialist trade association representing the world of outdoor events. Membership includes civic authorities, show organisers, event management companies, promoters and suppliers of equipment and services together with practitioners in general. The association publishes a members' yearbook and the NOEA code of practice for outdoor events. Copies upon application to the General Secretary. The association encourages good professional standards and practice in the industry.

National Outdoor Events Association
7 Hamilton Way, Wallington, Surrey SM6 9NJ
Tel: 0181 669 8121

SPECIAL EVENTS

International Special Events Society (ISES)
ISES was founded 10 years ago by Martin A J Van Keken, Jr to bring together all areas of expertise in the events industry and is the only such group existing today. The group organises workshops and forums to discuss issues such as world event standards and terminology, open and fair trade practices, environmental standards in event production, professional conduct and ethics, strategic alliances and global mergers.

ISES
Tel.: 001 604 708 0085

courtesy of Elegant Days

courtesy of Circo Rum Ba Ba
top left - Satanya & Bella Ze Bub
bottom left - Noriko & Akiko
centre top - The Leftover Linguini Sisters
centre - Sci-Fi Aliens
centre bottom - Crimplene & Cake
top right - Fats and Toots
bottom right - Neptune & Persephone

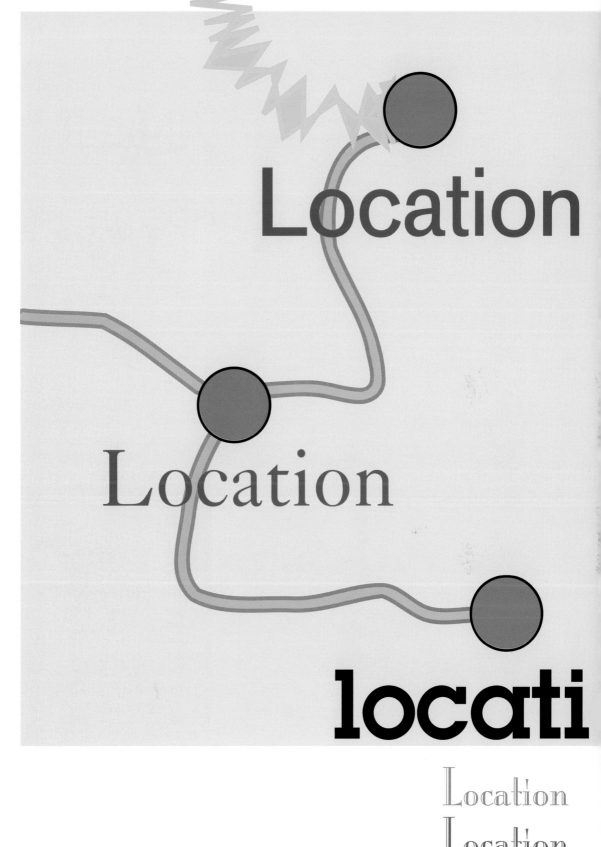

Location

Location

locati

Location
Location
Location

England & Wales

NORTHUMBERLAND

T.&W.

CUMBRIA

DURHAM

NORTH YORKS.

LANCS.

WEST YORKS.

EAST RID.

Ms.

GM.

S.YORKS.

CON.

DEN.

F.

CHESH.

DERBS.

NOTTS

LINCS

GWYND.

SHROPS.

STAFFS.

CERDGN.

POWYS

W.M.

WARWICKS.

LEICS.

R.

NORFOLK

PEM.

CARM.

HERES.

WORCS.

NORTHANTS.

CAMBS

SUFFOLK

GLAM.

M.

GLOUCS.

OXON

BEDS.

HERTS.

ESSEX

L.

SOMERSET

WILTS.

BERKS.

SURREY

KENT

CORNWALL

DEVON

DORSET

HANTS.

W.SUSSEX

E. SUSSEX

Scotland

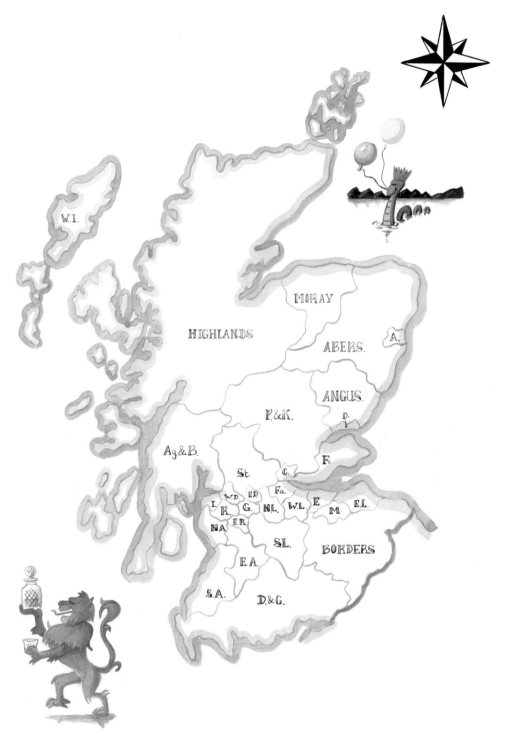

W.I.

HIGHLANDS

MORAY

ABERS.

A.

ANGUS.

P.&K.

D.

Ag&B.

F.

St.

C.

WD

ED

Fa.

I

R.

G.

NL.

W.L.

E

M

E.L.

NA

ER

S.L.

BORDERS

E.A.

S.A.

D.&G.

The West Country

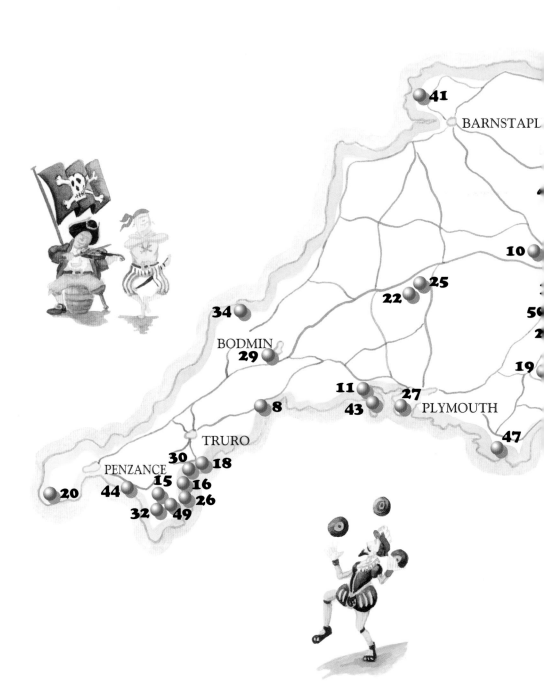

41

BARNSTAPL

10

25

22

34

BODMIN
29

11

27

43

PLYMOUTH

8

47

19

50

TRURO

30

18

PENZANCE

15

16

20

44

26

32

49

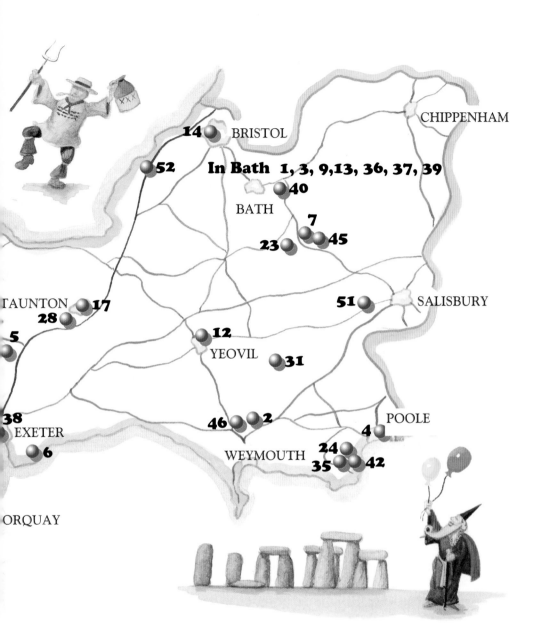

14 BRISTOL

52

In Bath 1, 3, 9,13, 36, 37, 39

40

BATH

7

45

23

TAUNTON **17**

28

5

51 SALISBURY

12

YEOVIL

31

38

EXETER

6

46 **2**

WEYMOUTH

POOLE

4

24

35 **42**

ORQUAY

The South East

READING

WINDSOR

7

16
31 63
32 55 22 50
59

41 42
30

66

46

47 56

58

BASINGSTOKE

67

25

3 35

26

51 15

21

GUILDFORD

1

33

4

WINCHESTER

54

65

64

SOUTHAMPTON

10

36

37 68 6 2

60

PORTSMOUTH

13 8 53

COWES

20

2

23

17

40

49

MAIDSTONE

19

CANTERBURY

45

12

57

24

DOVER

5 38

44 39

27

52

FOLKESTONE

RAWLEY

11

28

43

9 34

4

29

BRIGHTON

HASTINGS

EASTBOURNE

London

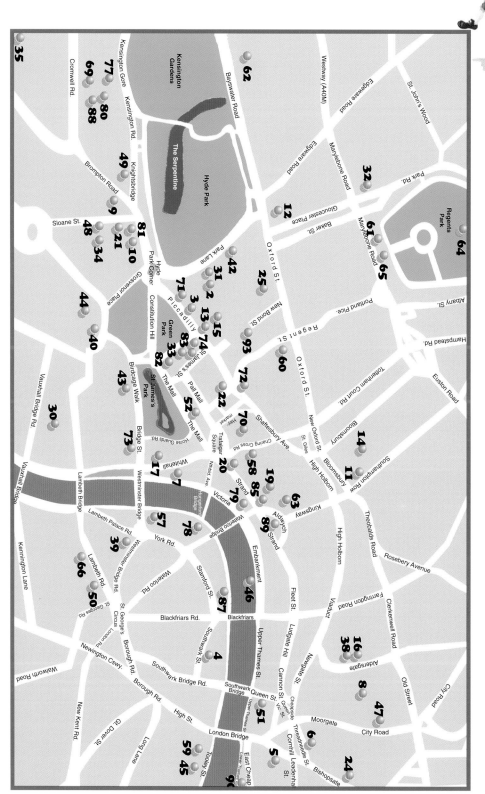
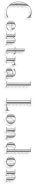

132

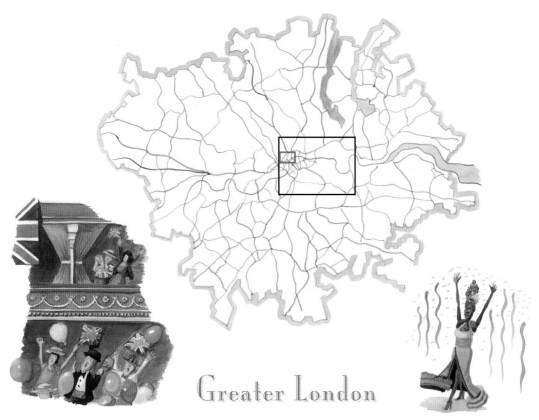

Greater London

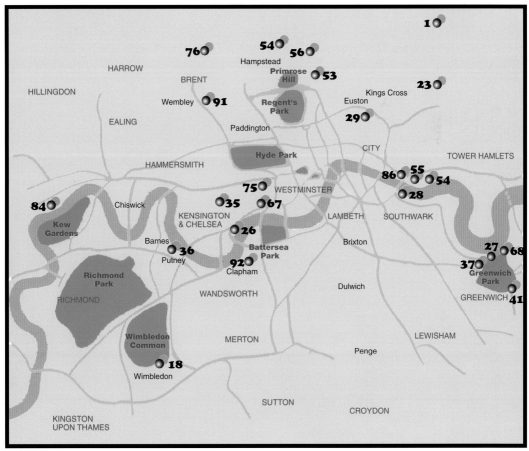

1

76 54 56
HARROW   Hampstead
                    Primrose
                    Hill   53
HILLINGDON   BRENT
                              Kings Cross   23
              Wembley 91   Euston
EALING   Regent's
                    Park   29
              Paddington

                    Hyde Park   CITY   TOWER HAMLETS
HAMMERSMITH
                    75 WESTMINSTER   86 55 54
84   Chiswick   35 67   28
Kew   KENSINGTON   LAMBETH   SOUTHWARK
Gardens   & CHELSEA
              Barnes   26   Brixton
                    36   Battersea   27 68
              Putney   Park   37
Richmond   92 Clapham   Dulwich   Greenwich
Park   RICHMOND   WANDSWORTH   Park
                                                GREENWICH 41

              Wimbledon   LEWISHAM
              Common
                    18   MERTON   Penge
              Wimbledon

KINGSTON   SUTTON   CROYDON
UPON THAMES

East Anglia

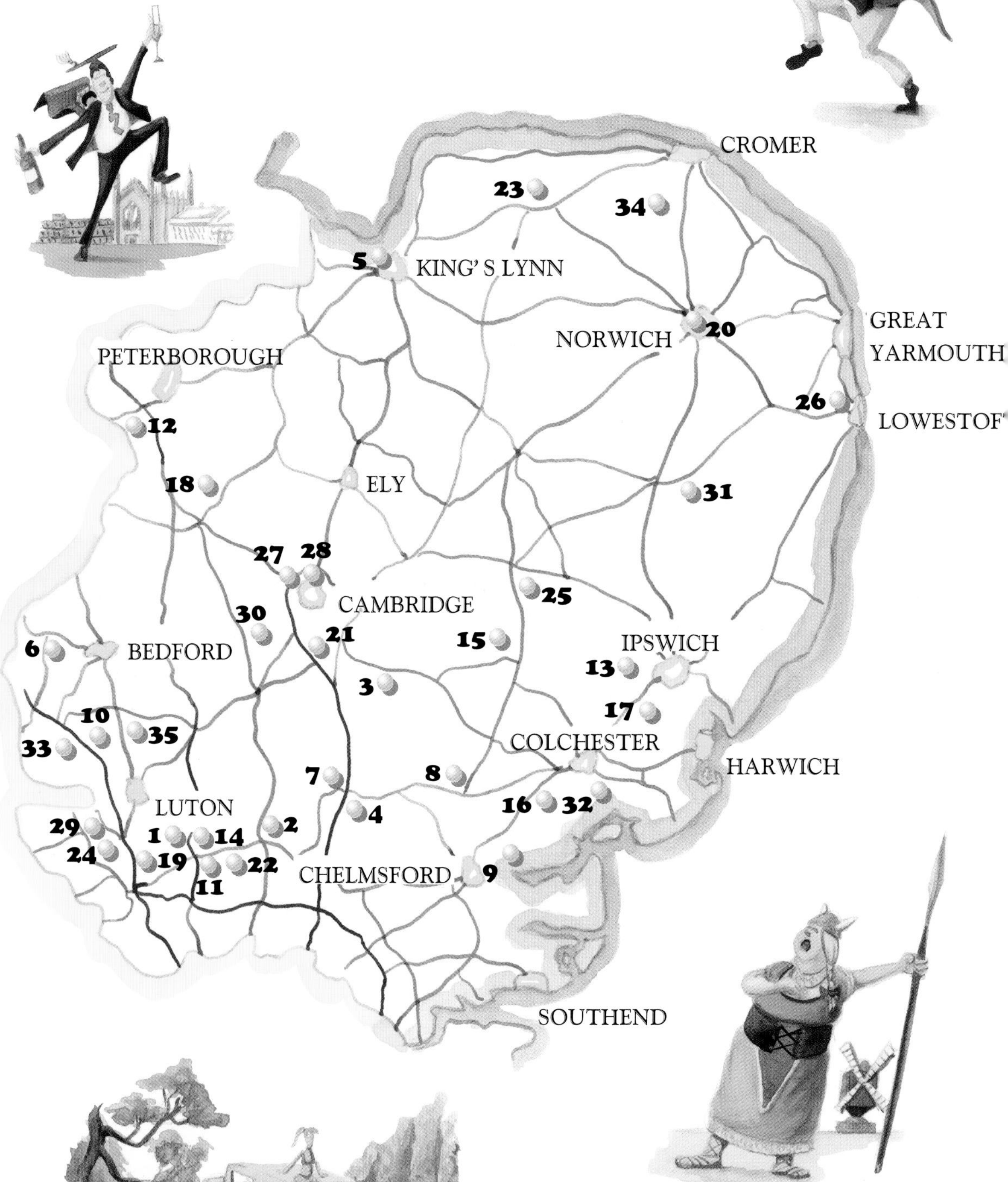

CROMER

23

34

5 KING'S LYNN

NORWICH 20

GREAT YARMOUTH

PETERBOROUGH

26

LOWESTOFT

12

18

ELY

31

27 28

25

30 CAMBRIDGE

6

BEDFORD

21

IPSWICH

15

13

3

17

10

35

COLCHESTER

33

HARWICH

7

8

16 32

LUTON

4

29

1 14

2

24

19 22

11 CHELMSFORD 9

SOUTHEND

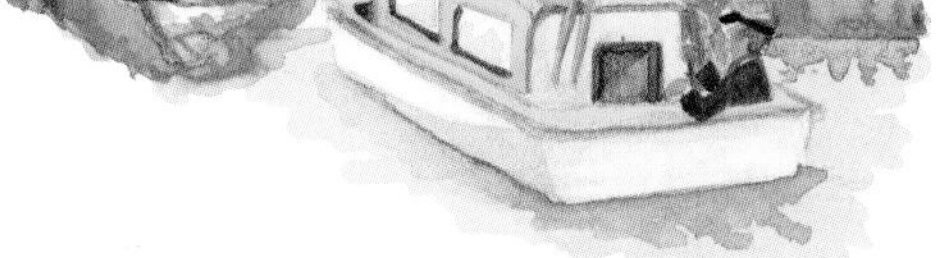

Central England

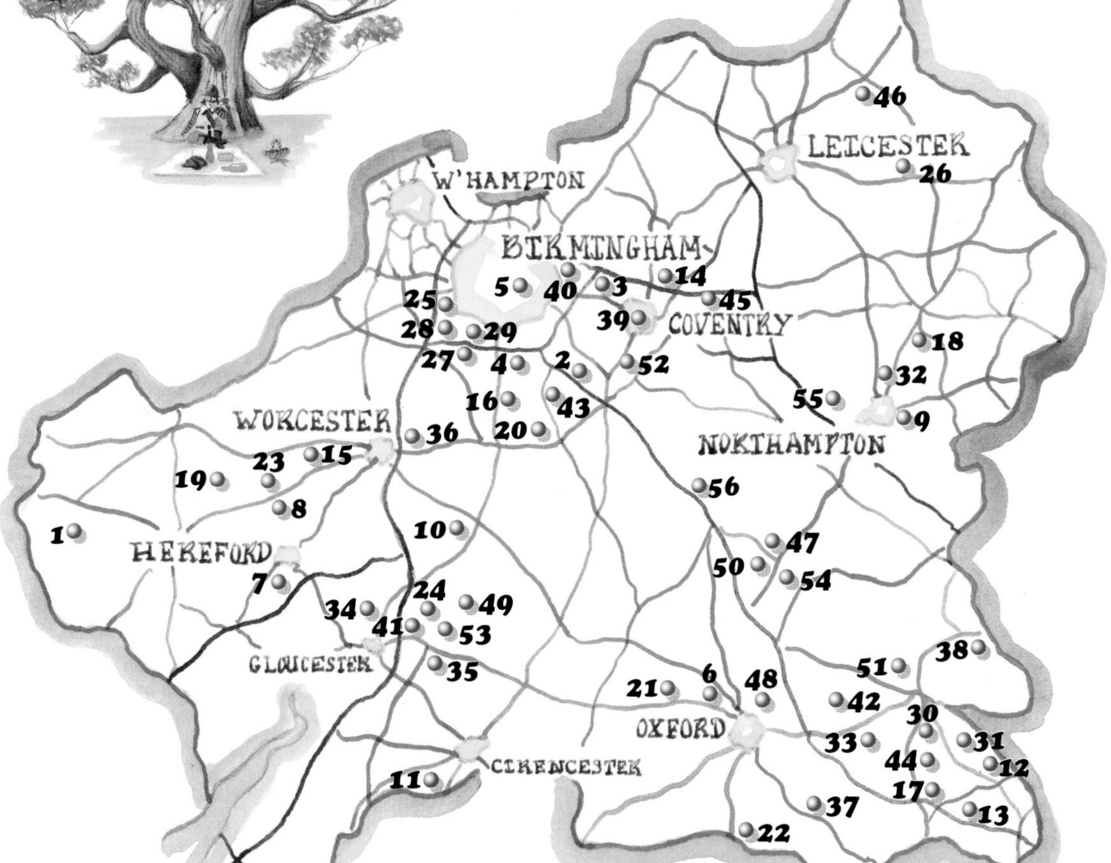

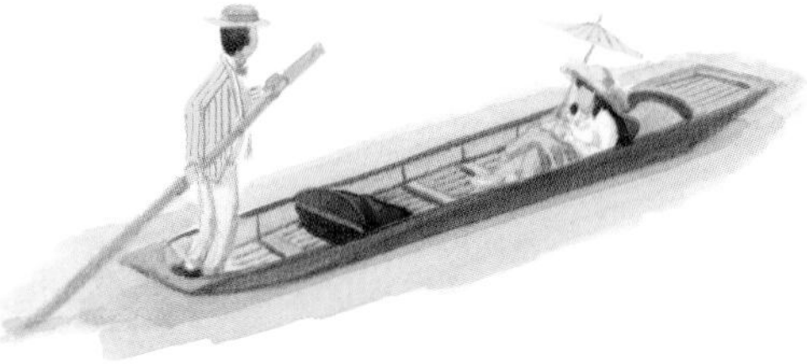

W'HAMPTON

BIRMINGHAM

25
28
27
29
4
16
20
36
43
2
52

5
40
3
14
45
39
COVENTRY

LEICESTER
46
26

WORCESTER
23
15
19
8
HEREFORD
7
10
34
41
24
49
53
35
GLOUCESTER
11
CIRENCESTER

18
32
9
55
NORTHAMPTON
56

47
50
54

21
6
48
OXFORD
22
37
51
42
33
30
44
17
38
31
12
13

Wales

HOLYHEAD

LLANDUDNO

4

13 3
25 14

22
WREXHAM
24

20 18

DOLGELLAU

WELSHPOOL

16

21
ABERYSTWYTH 1
8

LLANDRINDOD
WELLS

10

FISHGUARD

HAVERFORDWEST
19
11
9 2

12

15 23
17 6
5
SWANSEA
7 CARDIFF

The North West

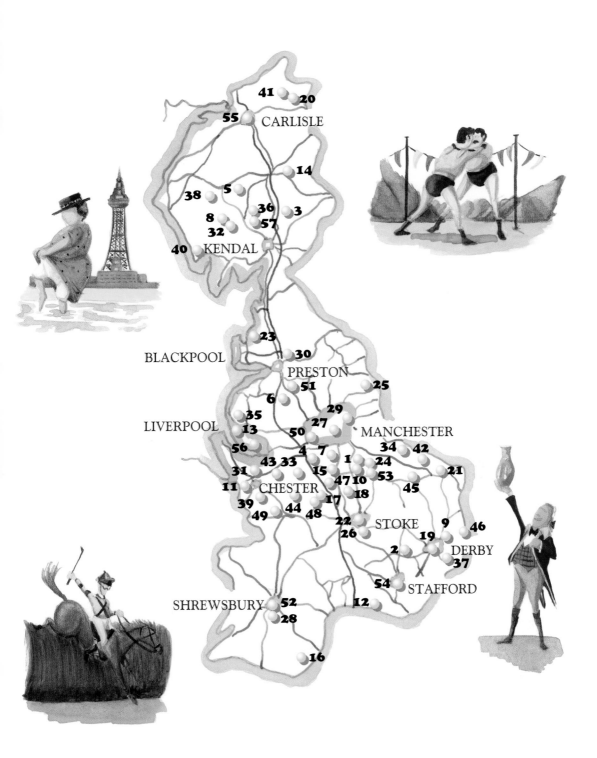

41   20

55   CARLISLE

14

38   5

36   3

8   57

32

40   KENDAL

23

BLACKPOOL

30

PRESTON

51   25

6

35   29

LIVERPOOL   27

13

50

MANCHESTER

56   4   7

34   42

43   33   1

24   21

31   15   53

11   47   10   45

CHESTER   18

39

44   48   STOKE   9   46

49   17

22   19

26   2   DERBY

37

54   STAFFORD

SHREWSBURY   52   12

28

16

The North East

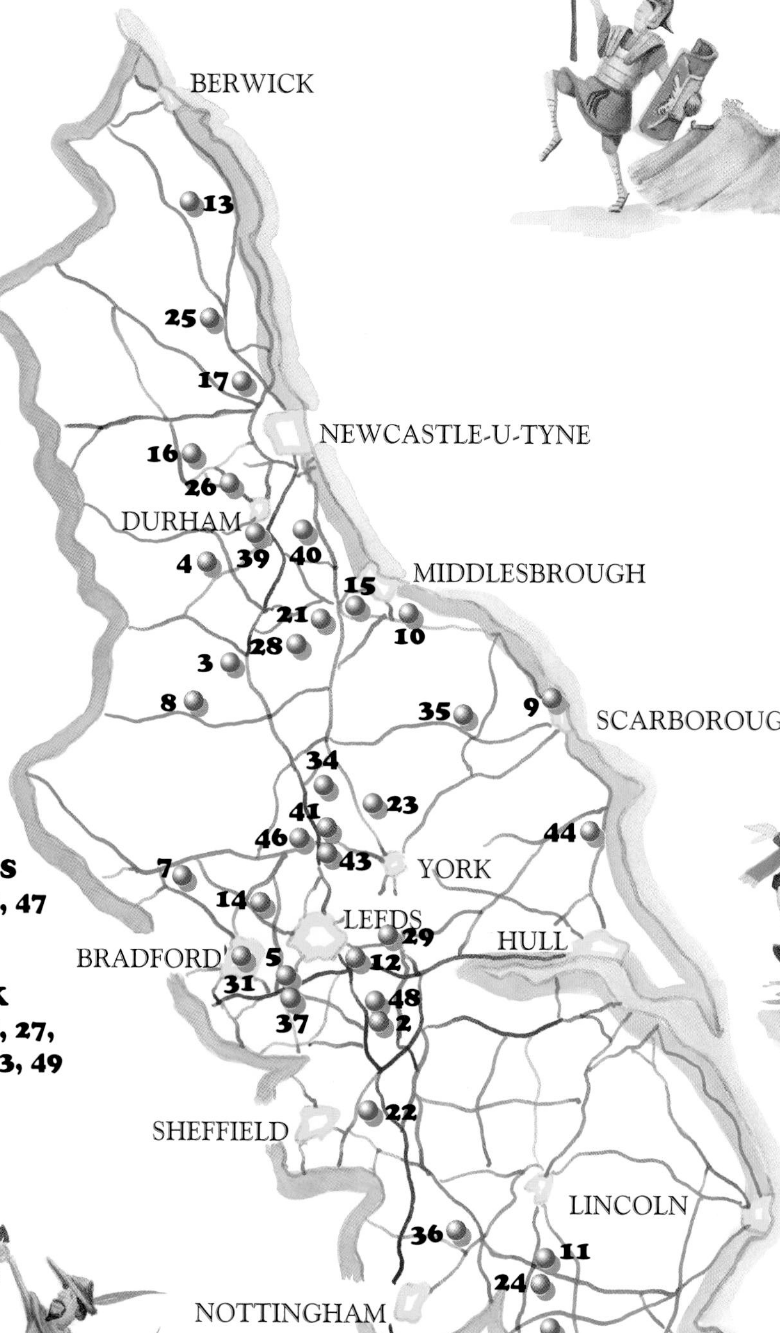

BERWICK

●13

25●

17●

NEWCASTLE-U-TYNE

16●
26●
DURHAM
4● 39● 40●
15●
MIDDLESBROUGH
21● 10●
28●
3●
8●
35● 9●
SCARBOROUGH

34●
41● 23●
46● 44●
7● 43●
YORK
14●
LEEDS
BRADFORD 5● 29●
12● HULL
31●
48●
37● 2●

22●
SHEFFIELD

LINCOLN
36●
SKEGNESS
11●
24●
NOTTINGHAM
45● 20●

In LEEDS
1, 38, 42, 47

In YORK
6, 18, 19, 27,
30, 32, 33, 49

Scotland

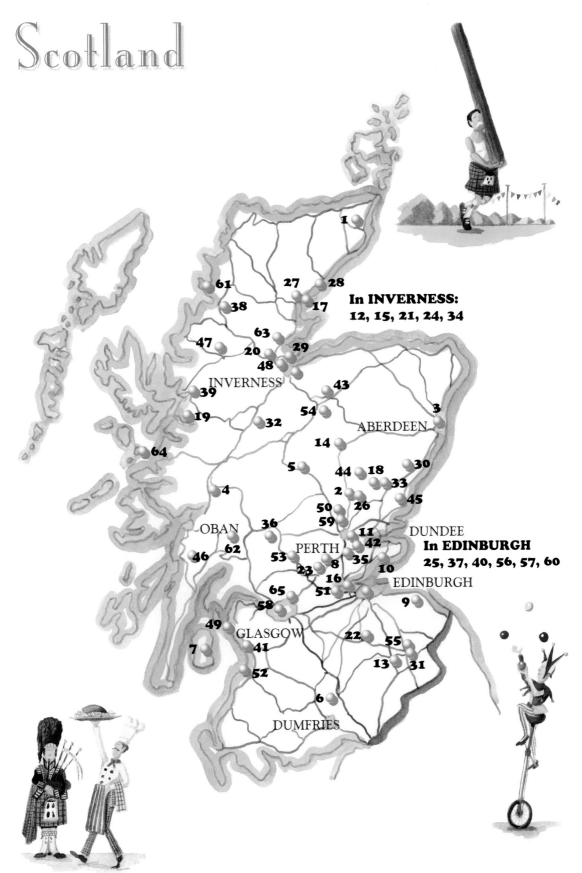

1

61 27 28

38 17

In INVERNESS:
12, 15, 21, 24, 34

63

47 20 29

48

INVERNESS

39 43

19 32

ABERDEEN

54

3

14

5 44 18 30

2 33

4 26 45

50

59

36 11 DUNDEE

OBAN 42

62 53 PERTH 35 In EDINBURGH

46 23 8 25, 37, 40, 56, 57, 60

16 10

65 51 EDINBURGH

58 9

49

GLASGOW 22 55

7 41

13 31

52

6

DUMFRIES

Key: **H - Hotel**
          SH - Stately Home
          CHH - Country House Hotel
          Misc - See name

Region 1 See map on pages 128 & 129

Abbey Hotel
North Parade   Map Ref **1**
Bath BA1 1LG
Tel: 01225 461603   H

Athelhampton House & Gardens
Athelhampton   Map Ref **2**
Dorchester
Dorset BT2 7LG
Tel: 01305 848363   SH

Bath Spa Hotel
Sydney Road   Map Ref **3**
Bath
Avon BA2 6JF
Tel: 01225 444424   H

Belvedere Hotel
Bath Road   Map Ref **4**
Bournemouth
Dorset BH1 2EU
Tel: 01202 297556   H

Bickleigh Castle
Bickleigh   Map Ref **5**
Nr Tiverton
Devon EX16 8RP
Tel: 01884 855363   Misc

Bicton Park
East Budleigh   Map Ref **6**
Budleigh Salterton
Devon EX9 7DP
Tel: 01935 568465   Misc

Bishopstrow House
Warminster   Map Ref **7**
Wiltshire BA12 9HH
Tel: 01985 212312   CHH

Caerhays Castle & Gardens
Gorran   Map Ref **8**
St Austell PL26 6LY
Tel: 01827 501310   Misc

Combe Grove Manor Hotel & Country Club
Brassknocker Hill   Map Ref **9**
Monkton Combe
Bath BA2 7HS
Tel: 01225 834644   CHH

Combe House Country Hotel
Gittisham   Map Ref **10**
Honiton
Devon EX14 0AD
Tel: 01404 42756   CHH

Combe House Country Hotel

Cotehele
St Dominick   Map Ref **11**
Nr Saltash PL12 6TA
Tel: 01579 351346   SH

Fleet Air Museum
RNAS Yeovilton   Map Ref **12**
Ilchester
Yeovil
Somerset BA22 8HT
Tel: 01935 840077   Misc

The Francis Hotel
Queen Square   Map Ref **13**
Bath
Avon BA1 2HH
Tel: 01225 424257   H

Glass Boat Restaurant
Welsh Back   Map Ref **14**
Nr Bristol Bridge
Bristol BS1 4SB
Tel: 0117 929 0704   Misc

Godolphin House
Godolphin Cross   Map Ref **15**
Helston
Cornwall TR13 9RE
Tel: 01736 762409   SH

Greenbank Hotel
Harbourside   Map Ref **16**
Falmouth
Cornwall TR11 2SR
Tel: 01326 312440   H

Hatch Court
Hatch Beauchamp   Map Ref **17**
Taunton
Somerset TA3 6AA
Tel: 01823 480120   Misc

Idle Rocks Hotel
The Harbourside   Map Ref **18**
St Mawes
Cornwall TR2 5AN
Tel: 01326 270771   H

Kingston House
Staverton   Map Ref **19**
Totnes
Devon TQ9 6AR
Tel: 01803 762235   SH

The Land's End
Duchy of Cornwall   Map Ref **20**
Cornwall TR19 7AA
Tel: 01736 871844   H

Langstone Cliff Hotel
Dawlish Warren   Map Ref **21**
Dawlish
Devon EX7 0NA
Tel: 01626 865155   H

Lewtrenchard Manor
Lewdown   Map Ref **22**
Nr Okehampton
Devon EX20 4PN
Tel: 01566 783256   H

Longleat
The Estate Office   Map Ref **23**
Warminster
Wiltshire BA12 7NW
Tel: 01985 844400   SH

Lulworth Castle
The Lulworth Estate   Map Ref **24**
East Lulworth
Wareham
Dorset BH20 5QS
Tel: 01929 400352   SH

Lulworth Castle

Lydford House Hotel
Okehampton   Map Ref **25**
Devon EX20 4AU
Tel: 01822 820347   H

Meudon Hotel
Mawnan Smith   Map Ref **26**
Falmouth
Cornwall TR11 5HT
Tel: 01326 250541   CHH

Mount Edgcumbe House & Country Park
Cremyll   Map Ref **27**
Torpoint PL10 1HZ
Tel: 01752 822236   CHH

The Old Municipal Buildings
Corporation Street   Map Ref **28**
Taunton
Somerset TA1 4AQ
Tel: 01823 335166   Misc

Pencarrow
Washaway   Map Ref **29**
Bodmin
Cornwall PL30 3AG
Tel: 01208 841369   SH

Penmere Manor
Mongleath Road   Map Ref **30**
Falmouth
Cornwall TR11 4PN
Tel: 01326 211411   CHH

Plumber Manor
Sturminster Newton   Map Ref **31**
Dorset DT10 2AF
Tel: 01258 472507   SH

Polurrian Hotel
Polurrian Lane   Map Ref **32**
Mullion
Helston
Cornwall TR12 7EN
Tel: 01326 240421   H

Powderham Castle
Powderham   Map Ref **33**
Exeter
Devon EX6 8JQ
Tel: 01626 890243   SH

Prideaux Place
Padstow   Map Ref **34**
Cornwall PL28 8RP
Tel: 01841 532411   SH

Priory Hotel
Church Green   Map Ref **35**
Wareham
Dorset BH20 4ND
Tel: 01929 551666   CHH

Priory Hotel
Weston Road   Map Ref **36**
Bath
Avon BA1 2XT
Tel: 01225 331922   H

Pump Room & Roman Baths
Stall Street   Map Ref **37**
Bath
Avon BA1 1LZ
Tel: 01225 477000   Misc

Royal Albert Memorial Museum
Queen Street   Map Ref **38**
Exeter EX4 3RX
Tel: 01392 265858   Misc

Royal Crescent
16 Royal Crescent   Map Ref **39**
Bath
Somerset BA1 2LS
Tel: 01225 739955   H

Royal Crescent

Rudloe Hall Hotel
Leafy Lane   Map Ref **40**
Box
Wiltshire SN13 0PA
Tel: 01225 810555   H

Saunton Sands Hotel
Saunton   Map Ref **41**
Braunton
Devon EX33 1LQ
Tel: 01271 890212   H

Smedmore House
Kimmeridge   Map Ref **42**
Wareham
Dorset BH20 5PG
Tel: 01929 480719   SH

St Mellion Hotel, Golf & Country Club
St Mellion   Map Ref **43**
Saltash
Cornwall PL12 6SD
Tel: 01579 351351   CHH

St Michael's Mount
Marazion   Map Ref **44**
Nr Penzance
Cornwall
Tel: 01736 710507   SH

Stourhead
Stourton   Map Ref **45**
Warminster BA12 6QD
Tel: 01747 841152   SH

Summer Lodge
Evershot   Map Ref **46**
Dorchester
Dorset DT2 0NG
Tel: 01935 83424   H

Tides Reach Hotel
South Sands   Map Ref **47**
Salcombe
Devon TQ8 8LJ
Tel: 01548 843466   H

Tiverton Castle
Tiverton   Map Ref **48**
Devon
EX16 6RP
Tel: 01884 253200   SH

Trelowarren House & Chapel
Mawgan-in-Meneage   Map Ref **49**
Helston
Cornwall TR12 6AD
Tel: 01326 221366   SH

Ugbrooke Hall
Chudleigh   Map Ref **50**
Devon TQ13 0AD
Tel: 01626 852179   Misc

Wilton House
The Estate Office   Map Ref **51**
Wilton
Salisbury SP2 0BJ
Tel: 01722 746720   SH

The Winter Gardens
Royal Parade   Map Ref **52**
Weston-Super-Mare
Avon BS23 1AQ
Tel: 01934 417117   Misc

Region 2 See map on pages 130 & 131

Alton Grange Hotel
Alton   Map Ref **1**
Hampshire GU34 4EG
Tel: 01420 86565   H

Amberley Castle
Nr Arundel   Map Ref **2**
West Sussex BN18 9ND
Tel: 01798 831992   CHH

Amberley Castle

Angel Posting House & Livery
91 High Street   Map Ref **3**
Guildford
Surrey GU1 3DP
Tel: 01483 564555   H

Anne of Cleves House
52 Southover High Street   Map Ref **4**
Lewes
Sussex BN7 1LA
Tel: 01273 474610   SH

Ashdown Park Hotel
Wych Cross   Map Ref **5**
Nr East Grinstead
East Sussex RH18 5JR
Tel: 01342 824988   CHH

Bailiffscourt
Climping   Map Ref **6**
West Sussex BN17 5RW
Tel: 01903 723511   CHH

Basildon Park
Lower Basildon   Map Ref **7**
Reading RG8 9NR
Tel: 0118 984 3040   SH

Beaulieu Estate
John Montague Building   Map Ref **8**
Brockenhurst
Hampshire SO42 7ZN
Tel: 01590 612345   SH

Bentley House & Gardens
Halland   Map Ref **9**
Nr Lewes
East Sussex BN8 5AF
Tel: 01825 840573   SH

Botley Park
Winchester Road   Map Ref **10**
Boorley Green
Botley
Hampshire SO32 2UA
Tel: 01489 780888   CHH

Buxted Park Hotel
Uckfield   Map Ref **11**
East Sussex TN22 4AY
Tel: 01825 732711   H

Chaucer Hotel
63 Ivy Lane   Map Ref **12**
Canterbury
Kent CT1 1TT
Tel: 01227 464427   H

Chewton Glen
Christchurh Road   Map Ref **13**
New Milton
Hampshire BH25 6QS
Tel: 01425 275341   CHH

Chewton Glen

Cisswood House Hotel
Sandygate Lane   Map Ref **14**
Lower Beeding
Nr Horsham
West Sussex RH13 6NF
Tel: 01403 891216   H

Clandon Park
West Clandon   Map Ref **15**
Guildford
Surrey GU4 7RQ
Tel: 01483 222482   SH

The Cliveden
Taplow   Map Ref **16**
Berkshire SL6 0JF
Tel: 01628 668561   CHH

Cliveden

Cobham Hall
Cobham   Map Ref **17**
Nr Gravesend
Kent DA12 3BL
Tel: 01474 823371/824319 SH

Coulsden Manor Hotel
Coulsden Court Road   Map Ref **18**
Coulsden
Croydon
Surrey CR5 2LL
Tel: 0181 668 0414   H

County Hotel
High Street   Map Ref **19**
Canterbury
Kent CT1 2RX
Tel: 01227 766266   H

Croydon Clocktower
Croydon   Map Ref **20**
Surrey CR9 1ET
Tel: 0181 253 1038   Misc

Denbies Wine Estate
London Road   Map Ref **21**
Dorking
Surrey RH5 6AA
Tel: 01306 876616   Misc

Dorney Court
Dorney   Map Ref **22**
Nr Windsor
Berkshire SL4 6QP
Tel: 01628 604638   SH

Down House
Downe   Map Ref **23**
Kent BR6 7JT
Tel: 01689 589119   SH

Eastwell Manor
Broughton Lees   Map Ref **24**
Ashford
Kent TN25 4HR
Tel: 01233 219955   CHH

Elvetham Hall Conference Centre
Hartley Wintney   Map Ref **25**
Basingstoke
Hampshire RG27 8AR
Tel: 01252 844871   Misc

Esseborne Manor
Hurstbourne Tarrant   Map Ref **26**
Nr Andover
Hampshire SP11 0ER
Tel: 01264 736444   H

Finchcocks
Goudhurst   Map Ref **27**
Kent TN17 1HH
Tel: 01580 211702   SH

Firle Place
Nr Lewes   Map Ref **28**
East Sussex BN8 6LP
Tel: 01273 858188   SH

Flackley Ash Hotel
Peasmarsh   Map Ref **29**
Rye
East Sussex TN31 6YH
Tel: 01797 230651   H

Foley Lodge Hotel
Stockcross   Map Ref **30**
Newbury
Berkshire RG20 8JU
Tel: 01635 528770   H

Fredrick's Hotel
Shoppenhangers Road   Map Ref **31**
Maidenhead
Berkshire SL6 2PZ
Tel: 01628 35934   H

French Horn Hotel
Sonning on Thames   Map Ref **32**
Berkshire RG4 6TN
Tel: 0118 969 2204   H

Gatton Manor Hotel
Standon Lane   Map Ref **33**
Ockley
Surrey RH5 5PQ
Tel: 01306 627555   CHH

Glynde Place
Glynde   Map Ref **34**
Lewes
East Sussex BN8 6SX
Tel: 01273 858224   SH

Goddards
Abinger Common   Map Ref **35**
Dorking
Surrey RH5 6TH
Tel: 01628 825920   SH

Goodwood House
Goodwoord   Map Ref **36**
Chichester
West Sussex PO18 0PX
Tel: 01243 755040   SH

Goodwood Park Hotel
Goodwood   Map Ref **37**
Chichester
West Sussex PO18 0QB
Tel: 01243 775537   CHH

Gravetye Manor
Vowels Lane   Map Ref **38**
Nr East Grinstead
West Sussex RH19 4LJ
Tel: 01342 810567   CHH

Groombridge Place Gardens
Groombridge   Map Ref **39**
Nr Royal Tunbridge Wells
Kent TN3 9QG
Tel: 01892 863999   SH

Hever Castle
Nr Edenbridge   Map Ref **40**
Kent TN8 7NG
Tel: 01732 865224   SH

Highclere Castle
Nr Newbury   Map Ref **41**
Berkshire RG20 9RN
Tel: 01635 253210   SH

Hollington Country House
Woolton Hill   Map Ref **42**
Newbury
Berkshire RG20 9XA
Tel: 01635 255100   CHH

Horstead Place
Little Horstead   Map Ref **43**
East Sussex TN22 5TS
Tel: 01825 750581   CHH

Hotel Du Vin & Bistro
Crescent Road   Map Ref **44**
Tunbridge Wells
Kent TN1 2LY
Tel: 01892 526455   H

Howfield Manor
Chartham Hatch   Map Ref **45**
Canterbury
Kent CT4 7HQ
Tel: 01227 738294   H

Kew Gardens
Royal Botanic Gardens   Map Ref **46**
Richmond
Surrey TW9 3AB
Tel: 0181 940 1171   Misc

Lakeside Country Club
Wharf Road   Map Ref **47**
Camberley
Surrey GU16 6PT
Tel: 01252 836464   H

Langshott Manor
Langshott   Map Ref **48**
Horley
Surrey RH6 9LN
Tel: 01293 786680   H

Leeds Castle
Maidstone   Map Ref **49**
Kent ME17 1PL
Tel: 01622 765400   SH

Leeds Castle

Legoland
Windsor   Map Ref **50**
Berkshire SL4 5JJ
Tel: 01753 626100   Misc

Legoland

Loseley Park
Guildford   Map Ref **51**
Surrey GU3 1HS
Tel: 01483 304440   SH

Lympne Castle
Nr Hythe   Map Ref **52**
Kent CT21 4LQ
Tel: 01303 267571   SH

Master Builders House
Bucklers Hard   Map Ref **53**
Beaulieu
Hampshire SO42 7XB
Tel: 01590 616523   Misc

Mottisfont Abbey
Mottisfont   Map Ref **54**
Nr Romsey
Hampshire SO51 0LP
Tel: 01794 340757   SH

Monkey Island Hotel
Bray-on-Thames   Map Ref **55**
Maidenhead
Berkshire SL6 2EE
Tel: 01628 623400   H

Pennyhill Park & Country Club
London Road   Map Ref **56**
Bagshot
Surrey GU19 5ET
Tel: 01276 471774   H

Pennyhill Park

Penshurst Place & Gardens
Penshurst   Map Ref **57**
Nr Tonbridge
Kent TN11 8DG
Tel: 01892 870307   SH

Richmond Gate Hotel
Richmond Hill   Map Ref **58**
Richmond upon Thames
Surrey TW10 6RP
Tel: 0181 940 0061   H

The Royal Berkshire
London Road   Map Ref **59**
Sunninghill
Ascot
Berkshire SL5 0PP
Tel: 01344 27100   H

The Royal Pavilion
Brighton   Map Ref **60**
East Sussex BN1 1EE
Tel: 01273 290900   Misc

The Royal Pavilion

St Mary's House
Bramber   Map Ref **61**
West Sussex BN44 3WE
Tel: 01903 816205   SH

Selsdon Park Hotel
Addington Road   Map Ref **62**
Sanderstead
South Croydon
Surrey CR2 8YA
Tel: 0181 657 8811   CHH

Sir Christopher Wren's House
Thames Street   Map Ref **63**
Windsor
Berkshire SL4 1PX
Tel: 01753 861354   H

South Lodge
Lower Beeding   Map Ref **64**
Nr Horsham
West Sussex RH13 6PS
Tel: 01403 891711   CHH

Spread Eagle
South Street   Map Ref **65**
Midhurst
West Sussex GU29 9NH
Tel: 01730 816911   CHH

Thorpe Park
Staines Road   Map Ref **66**
Chertsey
Surrey KT16 8PN
Tel: 01932 569393   Misc

Tylney Hall
Rotherick   Map Ref **67**
Nr Hook
Hampshire RG27 9AZ
Tel: 01256 764881   H

West Dean Gardens
The Edward James Foundation   Map Ref **68**
Estate Office
Chichester
West Sussex PO18 0QZ
Tel: 01243 818210   SH

Region 3 See map on pages 132 & 133

Alexandra Palace
Wood Green   Map Ref **1**
London N22   SH

Ascott Mayfair
49 Hill Street   Map Ref **2**
Mayfair
London W1X 7FQ
Tel: 0171 499 6868   H

Athenaeum Hotel
116 Piccadilly   Map Ref **3**
London W1V 0BJ
Tel: 0171 499 3464   H

Balls Brothers at the Hop Cellars
24 Southwark Street   Map Ref **4**
London SE1
Tel: 0171 403 6851   Misc

The Baltic Exchange
38 St Mary Axe   Map Ref **5**
London EC3A 8BH
Tel: 0171 369 1626   Misc

Bank of England Museum
Threadneedle St   Map Ref **6**
London EC2
Tel: 0171 601 5793   Misc

Banqueting House
Whitehall   Map Ref **7**
London SW1A 2ER
Tel: 0171 839 7569   Misc

Barbican Centre
Barbican Lane   Map Ref **8**
London EC2Y 8DS
Tel: 0171 638 4141   Misc

Basil Street Hotel
Knightsbridge   Map Ref **9**
London SW3 1AH
Tel: 0171 581 311   H

The Berkley
Knightsbridge   Map Ref **10**
London SW1X 7RL
Tel: 0171 235 6000   H

Bloomsbury Park
126 Southampton Row   Map Ref **11**
London WC1B 5AD
Tel: 0171 430 0434   H

The Brewers Rooms
42 Portman Square   Map Ref **12**
London W1H 0BB
Tel: 0171 486 4831   Misc

British Academy of Film & Television Arts
195 Piccadilly   Map Ref **13**
London W1V 0LN
Tel: 0171 734 0022   Misc

British Museum
Great Russell Street   Map Ref **14**
London WC1B 3DG
Tel: 0171 636 1555   Misc

Brown's Hotel
Albemarle Street   Map Ref **15**
London W1A 4SW
Tel: 0171 493 6020   H

Butchers Hall
Bartholomew Close
London EC1   Map Ref **16**
Tel: 0171 600 5777   Misc

Cabinet War Rooms
King Charles Street   Map Ref **17**
London W1
Tel: 0171 930 6961   Misc

Cannizaro House
West Side   Map Ref **18**
Wimbledon Common
London SW19 4UE
Tel: 0181 879 1464   H

Centre Stage
Covent Garden   Map Ref **19**
London WC2
Tel: 0171 379 6009   Misc

Charing Cross Hotel
Strand   Map Ref **20**
London WC2N 5HX
Tel: 0171 839 7182   H

Chelsea Hotel
17 Sloane Street   Map Ref **21**
London SW1X 9NU
Tel: 0171 235 4377   H

The Cinema Suite
Planet Hollywood   Map Ref **22**
Picadilly W1
Tel: 0171 437 7827   Misc

Circus Space
Nr. Old Street   Map Ref **23**
London N1
Tel: 0181 682 4900   Misc

The City of London Club
19 Broad Street   Map Ref **24**
London EC2
Tel: 0171 588 7991   Misc

Claridge's
Mayfair   Map Ref **25**
London W1A 2JQ
Tel: 0171 629 8860   H

Conrad International London
Chelsea Harbour   Map Ref **26**
London SW10
Tel: 0171 823 3000   H

Cutty Sark Clipper Ship
King William Walk   Map Ref **27**
Greenwich
London SE10 9HT
Tel: 0181 858 2698   Misc

Design Museum
Butler's Wharf   Map Ref **28**
Shad Thames SE1
Tel: 0171 403 6933   Misc

Dickens House Museum
48 Doughty Street   Map Ref **29**
London WC1N 2LF
Tel: 0171 405 2127   Misc

Dolphin Square Hotel
Dolphin Square   Map Ref **30**
London SW1V 3LX
Tel: 0171 834 3800   H

The Dorchester
Park Lane   Map Ref **31**
London W1A 2HJ
Tel: 0171 629 8888   H

Dorset Square Hotel
39/40 Dorset Square   Map Ref **32**
London NW1 6QN
Tel: 0171 723 7874   H

Duke's Hotel
St James's Place   Map Ref **33**
London SW1A 1NY
Tel: 0171 491 4840   H

Durley House
115 Sloane Street   Map Ref **34**
London SW1X 9PJ
Tel: 0171 235 5537   H

Earls Court Olympia
Olympia Conference Centre   Map Ref **35**
Hammersmith Road
London W14 8UX
Tel: 0171 370 8532   Misc

Elizabethan Mississippi Paddle Steamer
3 The Mews   Map Ref **36**
6 Putney Common
London SW15 1HL
Tel: 0181 780 1562   Misc

Fan Museum
12 Croom's Hill   Map Ref **37**
Greenwich
London SE10 8ER
Tel: 0181 305 1441   Misc

Farmers & Fletchers Hall
3 Cloth Street   Map Ref **38**
London EC1A 7LD
Tel: 0171 600 2204   Misc

Florence Nightingale Museum Trust
3 Lambeth Palace Road   Map Ref **39**
London SE1 7EW
Tel: 0171 620 0374   Misc

Goring Hotel
Beeston Place   Map Ref **40**
London SW1W 0JW
Tel: 0171 396 9000   H

Greenwich Observatory
National Maritime Museum   Map Ref **41**
Romney Road
Greenwich SE10 9NF
Tel: 0181 858 4422   Misc

Grosvenor House Hotel
Park Lane   Map Ref **42**
London W1A 3AA
Tel: 0171 499 6363   H

Guards Museum
Wellington Barracks   Map Ref **43**
Birdcage Walk
London SW1E 6HQ
Tel: 0171 414 3428   Misc

Hatkin
Belgravia   Map Ref **44**
London SW1X 7DJ
Tel: 0171 333 1000   H

HMS Belfast
Morgans Lane   Map Ref **45**
Tooley Street
London SE1 2JH
Tel: 0171 403 6246   Misc

HMS Belfast

HMS Wellington
Temple Stairs   Map Ref **46**
Victoria Embankment
London EC2R 2PN
Tel: 0171 653 6666   Misc

Honourable Artillery Company
Armoury House   Map Ref **47**
City Road
London EC1Y 2BQ
Tel: 0171 382 1533   Misc

Hyatt Carlton Tower
Cadogan Place   Map Ref **48**
London SW1X 9PY
Tel: 0171 235 1234   H

Hyde Park Hotel
66 Knightsbridge   Map Ref **49**
London SW1Y 7LA
Tel: 0171 235 2000   H

Imperial War Museum
Lambeth Road   Map Ref **50**
London SE1 6HZ
Tel: 0171 416 5394   Misc

Imperial War Museum

Innholders' Hall
30 College St   Map Ref **51**
London EC4
Tel: 0171 236 7638   Misc

Institute of Contemporary Arts
The Mall   Map Ref **52**
London SW1Y 5AH
Tel: 0171 930 0493   Misc

Jongleurs
Middle Yard   Map Ref **53**
Camden Lock
London NW1 8AB
Tel: 0171 924 2248   Misc

Kenwood House
Hampstead Lane   Map Ref **54**
London NW3 7TR
Tel: 0181 348 1286   Misc

Lady Daphne
St Katherine's Dock   Map Ref **55**
London E1
Tel: 01273 890 328   Misc

Lauderdale House
Waterlow Park   Map Ref **56**
Highgate Hill
London N6 5HG
Tel: 0181 348 8716   Misc

London Aquarium
County Hall   Map Ref **57**
Westminster Bridge Road
London SE1
Tel: 0171 967 8000   Misc

London Astoria
157 Charing Cross Road   Map Ref **58**
London WC2H 0EN
Tel: 0171 434 9592   Misc

London Dungeon
Tooley Street   Map Ref **59**
London SE1 2SZ
Tel: 0171 403 7221   Misc

London Palladium
Argyll Street   Map Ref **60**
London W1
Tel: 0171 437 7373   Misc

London Planetarium
Marylebone Road   Map Ref **61**
London NW1 5LR
Tel: 0171 935 6861   Misc

London Planetarium

London Toy & Model Museum
21-23 Craven Hill   Map Ref **62**
London W2 3EN
Tel: 0171 706 8000   Misc

London Transport Museum
Covent Garden   Map Ref **63**
London WC2E 7BB
Tel: 0171 379 6344   Misc

London Zoo
Regent's Park   Map Ref **64**
London NW1 4RY
Tel: 0171 586 3910   Misc

Madam Tussauds
Marylebone Road   Map Ref **65**
London NW1 5LR
Tel: 0171 935 6861   Misc

Museum of Garden History
The Ark   Map Ref **66**
220 Lambeth Road
London SE1 3JY
Tel: 0171 633 97Tel: 01   Misc

National Army Museum
Royal Hospital Road   Map Ref **67**
Chelsea
London SW3 4HT
Tel: 0171 730 0717   Misc

National Maritime Museum
Romney Road   Map Ref **68**
Greenwich
London SE10 9EF
Tel: 0181 858 4422   Misc

Natural History Museum
Cromwell Road   Map Ref **69**
South Kensington SW7
Tel: 0171 938 9123   Misc

Natural History Museum

Notre Dame Hall
5/6 Leicester Place   Map Ref **70**
Leicester Square
London WC2H 7BP
Tel: 0171 437 5571   Misc

Park Lane Hotel
Piccadilly   Map Ref **71**
London W1Y 8BX
Tel: 0171 499 6321   H

Planet Hollywood
13 Coventry Street   Map Ref **72**
London W1V 7FE
Tel: 0171 437 7827   Misc

Queen Elizabeth II Conference Centre
Broad Sanctuary   Map Ref **73**
Westminster
London SW1P 3EE
Tel: 0171 798 4000   Misc

The Ritz
150 Piccadilly   Map Ref **74**
London W1V 9DG
Tel: 0171 493 8181   H

The Roof Gardens
99 Kensington High Street   Map Ref **75**
London W8 5ED
Tel: 0171 937 7994   Misc

Royal Air Force Museum
Grahams Park Way   Map Ref **76**
London NW9 5LL
Tel: 0181 205 2266   Misc

Royal Albert Hall
Kensington Gore   Map Ref **77**
London SW7 2AP
Tel: 0171 589 3203   Misc

Royal Festival Hall
South Bank Centre   Map Ref **78**
London SE1 8XX
Tel: 0171 921 0680   Misc

The Savoy
The Strand   Map Ref **79**
London WC2R 0EU
Tel: 0171 836 4343   H

The Savoy

The Science Museum
Exhibition Road   Map Ref **80**
London SW7 2DD
Tel: 0171 938 8008   Misc

Sheraton Park Tower
101 Knightsbridge   Map Ref **81**
London SW1X 7RN
Tel: 0171 235 8050   H

Spencer House
27 St James's Place   Map Ref **82**
London
SW1A 1NR
Tel: 0171 514 1964   Misc

St James's Club
7-8 Park Place   Map Ref **83**
London SW14 1LP
Tel: 0171 629 7688   Misc

Syon House
Brentford   Map Ref **84**
Middlesex TW8 8JF
Tel: 0181 560 0881   Misc

Theatre Museum
1E Tavistock Street   Map Ref **85**
London WC2E 7PA
Tel: 0171 835 7891   Misc

Tower Bridge
London SE1 2UP   Map Ref **86**
Tel: 0171 403 3761   Misc

Venice Simplon - Orient Express
Orient-Express Services   Map Ref **87**
20 Upper Ground
London SE1 9PF
Tel: 0171 928 6000   Misc

Victoria & Albert Museum
Cromwell Road   Map Ref **88**
South Kensington
London SW7 2RL
Tel: 0171 938 8500   Misc

Le Meridien Waldorf
Aldwych Map Ref **89**
London WC2B 4DD
Tel: 0171 836 2400 H

Watermen's Hall
16 St Mary at Hill Map Ref **90**
London EC3R 8EE
Tel: 0171 283 2373 Misc

Wembley Arena
Wembley Map Ref **91**
London HA9 0DW
Tel: 0181 902 8833 Misc

Wessex House
1A St John's Hill Map Ref **92**
London SW11
Tel: 0171 622 6818 Misc

The Westbury
Bond Street Map Ref **93**
London W1A 4UH
Tel: 0171 629 7755 H

White House
Albady Street Map Ref **94**
Regents Park
London NW1 3UP
Tel: 0171 387 1200 Misc

Region 4 See map on page 134

Brocket Hall
Welwyn Map Ref **1**
Hertfordshire AL8 7XG
Tel: 01707 335241 H

Byrches at the Priory
High Street Map Ref **2**
Ware
Hertfordshire SG12 9AL
Tel: 01920 486500 Misc

Chilford Halls
Balsham Road Map Ref **3**
Linton
Cambridgeshire CB16LE
Tel: 01223 892641 Misc

Chilford Halls

Churchgate Manor Hotel
Churchgate Street Village Map Ref **4**
Old Harlow
Essex CM17 0JT
Tel: 01279 420246 H

Congham Hall
Lynn Road Map Ref **5**
King's Lynn
Norfolk PE32 1AH
Tel: 01485 600250 CHH

Cowper & Newton Museum
Orchard Side Map Ref **6**
Market Place
Olney MK46 4AJ
Tel: 01234 711516 Misc

Down Hall Country House Hotel
Hatfield Heath Map Ref **7**
Bishops Stortford
Hertfordshire CM22 7AS
Tel: 01279 731441 H

The Fennes Estate
Fennes Road Map Ref **8**
Braintree
Essex CM7 5PL
Tel: 01376 324555 Misc

Five Lakes Hotel Golf & Country Club
Colchester Road Map Ref **9**
Tolleshunt Knights
Essex CM9 8HX
Tel: 01621 868888 CHH

Flitwick Manor
Church Road Map Ref **10**
Flitwick
Bedfordshire MK45 1AE
Tel: 01525 712242 CHH

Hatfield House
Hatfield Map Ref **11**
Hertfordshire AL9 5NQ
Tel: 01707 272738 SH

Haycock Hotel
Wansford Map Ref **12**
Cambridgeshire PE8 6JA
Tel: 01780 782223 H

Hintlesham Hall Hotel
George Street Map Ref **13**
Hintlesham
Suffolk IP8 3NS
Tel: 01473 652334 CHH

Homestead Court Hotel
Welwyn Garden City Map Ref **14**
Hertfordshire AL7 4LK
Tel: 01707 324336 H

Kentwell Hall
Long Melford Map Ref **15**
Suffolk CO10 9BA
Tel: 01787 310207 SH

Layer Marney Tower
Nr Colchester Map Ref **16**
Essex CO5 9US
Tel: 01206 330784 Misc

Maison Talbooth
Stratford Road Map Ref **17**
Dedham
Essex CO7 6HP
Tel: 01206 323150 CHH

Maison Talbooth

The Manor
Hemingford Grey Map Ref **18**
Huntingdon
Camridgeshire PE18 9BN
Tel: 01480 463134 SH

The Manor
St Michaels Village Map Ref **19**
Fishpool Street
St Albans
Hertfordshire AL3 4RY
Tel: 01727 864444 Misc

Norwich Castle Museum
Castle Meadow Map Ref **20**
Norwich
Norfolk NR1 3JU
Tel: 01603 223628 Misc

Officers' Mess Conference Centre
Imperial War Museum Map Ref **21**
Duxford
Cambridgeshire CB2 4QR
Tel: 01223 833686 Misc

The Old Palace
Hatfield Park Map Ref **22**
Hatfield
Hertfordshire AL10 0HA
Tel: 01707 262055 Misc

The Old Rectory
Great Snoring Map Ref **23**
Fakenham
Norfolk NR21 0HP
Tel: 01328 820597 CHH

The Old Rectory

Pendley Manor Hotel
Cow Lane Map Ref **24**
Tring
Hertfordshire HP23 5QY
Tel: 01442 891891 H

Ravenwood Hall
Rougham Map Ref **25**
Bury St Edmunds
Suffolk IP30 9JA
Tel: 01359 270345 CHH

Somerleyton Hall & Gardens
Lowestoft Map Ref **26**
Suffolk NR32 5QQ
Tel: 01502 730224 SH

Trinity Hall
Trinity Lane Map Ref **27**
Cambridge
Cambridgeshire CB2 1TJ
Tel: 01223 332554 Misc

West Road Concert Hall
11 West Road Map Ref **28**
University Of Cambridge
Cambridgeshire C33 9DP
Tel: 01223 335184 Misc

Whipsnade Wild Animal Park
Whipsnade   Map Ref **29**
Dunstable
Bedfordshire LU6 2LF
Tel: 01582 872 171   Misc

Wimpole Hall
Arrington   Map Ref **30**
Royston SG8 0BW
Tel: 01223 207257   SH

Wingfield Old College & Gardens
Wingfield   Map Ref **31**
Nt Stradbroke
Suffolk IP21 5RA
Tel: 01379 384888   SH

Wivenhoe House Hotel
Wivenhoe Park   Map Ref **32**
Colchester
Essex CO4 2SQ
Tel: 01206 863666   H

Woburn Abbey
Woburn Estate   Map Ref **33**
Woburn
Bedfordshire MK17
Tel: 01252 290666   CHH

Wolterton Park
Erpingham   Map Ref **34**
Norfolk NR11 7BB
Tel: 01263 584175   SH

Wrest Park
Silsoe   Map Ref **35**
Bedfordshire MK17
Tel: 01525 860152   SH

Region 5 See map on page 135

Allt Yr Ynys
Waterstone   Map Ref **1**
Hertfordshire HR2 0DU
Tel: 01973 890307   CHH

Alveston Manor
Clopton Bridge   Map Ref **2**
Stratford-upon-Avon
Warwickshire CV37 7HP
Tel: 01789 204581   H

The Belfry
Wishaw   Map Ref **3**
Warwickshire B76 9PR
Tel: 01675 470301   CHH

Billesley Manor Hotel
Alcester   Map Ref **4**
Nr Stratford-upon-Avon
Warwickshire B49 6NF
Tel: 01789 400888   H

Birmingham Botanical Gardens &
Glasshouses   Map Ref **5**
Westbourne Road
Edgbaston
West Midlands B15 3TR
Tel: 0121 454 1860   Misc

Blenheim Palace
Woodstock   Map Ref **6**
Oxfordshire OX20 1PX
Tel: 01993 811325   SH

Brobury House & Garden
Brobury   Map Ref **7**
Nr Hereford
Herefordshire HR3 6BS
Tel: 01981 500229   SH

Burton Court
Eardisland   Map Ref **8**
Nr Leominster
Herefordshire HR6 9DN
Tel: 01544 388231   SH

Castle Ashby
Castle Ashby House   Map Ref **9**
Castle Ashby
Northampton NN7 1LQ
Tel: 01604 696696   SH

Charingworth Manor
Charingworth   Map Ref **10**
Nr Chipping Campden
Gloucestershire GL55 6NS
Tel: 01386 593555   H

Chavenage
Tetbury   Map Ref **11**
Gloucestershire GL8 8XP
Tel: 01666 502329   SH

Chenies Manor House
Chenies   Map Ref **12**
Buckinghamshire WD3 6ER
Tel: 01494 762888   SH

Chiltern Open Air Museum
Newland Park   Map Ref **13**
Gorelands Lane
Chalfont St. Giles
Buckinghamshire HP8 4AD
Tel: 01494 871117   SH

Coombe Abbey Hotel
Brinklow Road   Map Ref **14**
Binley
Coventry CV3 2AB
Tel: 01203 450450   H

Coombe Abbey Hotel

The Cottage in the Wood
Holywell Road   Map Ref **15**
Malvern Wells
Worcestershire WR14 4LG
Tel: 01684 575859   CHH

Coughton Court
Alcester   Map Ref **16**
Warwickshire B49 5JA
Tel: 01789 400777   SH

Danesfield House
Henley Road   Map Ref **17**
Marlow
Buckinghamshire SL7 2EY
Tel: 01682 891Tel: 010   CHH

Deene Park
Corby   Map Ref **18**
Northamptonshire
Tel: 01780 450278/450223 SH

The Elms
Abberley   Map Ref 19
Worcestershire WR6 6AT
Tel: 01299 896666   CHH

Ettington Park
Alderminster   Map Ref **20**
Stratford-upon-Avon
Warwickshire CV37 8BU
Tel: 01789 45Tel: 0123   CHH

The Feathers
Market Street   Map Ref **21**
Woodstock
Oxfordshire OX20 1SX
Tel: 01993 812291   H

The Feathers

Donnington Valley Hotel
Old Oxford Road   Map Ref **22**
Donnington
Newbury RG14 3AG
Tel: 01635 551123   H

Foley Arms Hotel
14 Worcester Road   Map Ref **23**
Malvern
Worcestershire WR14 4QS
Tel: 01684 573397   H

The Greenway
Shurdington   Map Ref **24**
Cheltenham
Gloucestershire GL51 5UG
Tel: 01242 862352   CHH

Hagley Hall
Stourbridge   Map Ref **25**
West Midlands DY9 9LG
Tel: 01562 882408   SH

Hambleton Hall
Hambleton   Map Ref **26**
Rutland LE15 8TH
Tel: 01572 756991   H

Hanbury Hall
Droitwich   Map Ref **27**
Worcestershire WR9 7EA
Tel: 01527 821214   SH

Harvington Hall
Kidderminster   Map Ref **28**
Worcester DY10 4LR
Tel: 01562 777846   SH

Hopton Court
Cleobury Mortimer   Map Ref **29**
Kidderminster
Herefordshire DY14 0EF
Tel: 01299 270734   SH

Hughenden Manor
High Wycombe   Map Ref **30**
Buckinghamshire HP14 4LA
Tel: 01494 532580   SH

Kew Bridge Steam Museum
Green Dragon Lane   Map Ref **31**
Brentford
Middlesex TW8 0EN
Tel: 0181 568 4757   Misc

Lamport Hall & Gardens
Lamport   Map Ref **32**
Northamptonshire NN6 9HD
Tel: 01604 686272   SH

Le Manoir aux Quat' Saisons
Church Road   Map Ref **33**
Great Milton
Oxfordshire OX44 7PD
Tel: 01844 278881   H

Littledean Hall
The Royal Forest of Dean Map Ref **34**
Gloucestershire GL14 3NR
Tel: 01594 824213   SH

Lords Of The Manor
Upper Slaughter   Map Ref **35**
Nr Bourton-on-the-Water
Gloucestershire GL54 2JD
Tel: 01451 820243   H

The Lygon Arms
Broadway   Map Ref **36**
Worcestershire WR12 7DU
Tel: 01386 852255   H

The Lygon Arms

Mapledurham House & Watermill
Mapledurham   Map Ref **37**
Oxfordshire RG4 7TR
Tel: 0118 972 3350   SH

Marriott Hanbury Manor Hotel
Ware   Map Ref **38**
Hertfordshire SG12 0SD
Tel: 01920 487722   CHH

Museum Of British Road Transport
St Agnes Lane   Map Ref **39**
Coventry
West Midlands CV1 1PN
Tel: 01203 823425   Misc

New Hall
Walmley Road   Map Ref **40**
Sutton Coldfield
West Midlands B76 1QX
Tel: 0121 378 2442   CHH

Owlpen Manor
Owlpen   Map Ref **41**
Gloucestershire GL11 5BZ
Tel: 01453 860261   SH

Pinewood Studios
Pinewood Road   Map Ref **42**
Buckinghamshire SL0 0NH
Tel: 01753 656953   Misc

Ragley Hall
Alcester   Map Ref **43**
Warwickshire B49 5NJ
Tel: 01789 762090   SH

Spread Eagle
Cornmarket   Map Ref **44**
Thame
Oxfordshire OX9 2BW
Tel: 01844 213661   H

Stanford Hall
Lutterworth   Map Ref **45**
Leicestershire LE17 6DH
Tel: 01788 860250   SH

Stapleford Park
Nr Melton Mowbray   Map Ref **46**
Leicestershire LE14 2EF
Tel: 01572 787522   CHH

Stapleford Park

Stowe Landscape Gardens
Buckingham   Map Ref **47**
Buckinghamshire MK18 5EH
Tel: 01280 822850   SH

Studley Priory
Horton-cum-Studley   Map Ref **48**
Oxfordshire OX33 1AZ
Tel: 01865 351203   H

Sudeley Castle
Winchcombe   Map Ref 49
Gloucestershire GL54 4JD
Tel: 01242 602308   SH

Villiers Hotel
3 Castle Street   Map Ref **50**
Buckingham
Buckinghamshire MK18 1BS
Tel: 01280 822444   H

Waddesdon Manor
Nr Aylesbury   Map Ref **51**
Buckinghamshire HP18 0JW
Tel: 01296 651211   SH

Warwick Castle
Warwick   Map Ref **52**
Warwickshire CV34 4QU
Tel: 01926 406600   SH

Washbourne Court
Lower Slaughter   Map Ref **53**
Cheltenham
Gloucestershire GL54 2HS
Tel: 01451 822143   CHH

Winslow Hall
Winslow   Map Ref **54**
Buckinghamshire MK18 3HL
Tel: 01296 712323   SH

Woodhouse at Princethorpe
Leamington Road   Map Ref **55**
Princethorpe
Nr Rugby
Warwickshire CV 23 9PZ
Tel: 01926 632131   H

Wroxton House Hotel
Wroxton St Mary   Map Ref **56**
Nr Banbury
Oxfordshire OX15 6QB
Tel: 01295 730777   H

Region 6 See map on page 136

Aberystwyth Arts Centre
Aberystwyth   Map Ref **1**
Ceredigion
Tel: 01970 622882   Misc

The Bear Hotel
Crickhowell NP8 1BW   Map Ref **2**
Tel: 01873 810408   H

Bodysgallen Hall
Llandudno   Map Ref **3**
Conway LL30 1RS
Tel: 01492 584466   CHH

Bryn Tirion Hotel
Red Wharf Bay   Map Ref **4**
Isle of Anglesey
Gwynedd LL75 8RZ
Tel: 01248 852366   H

Cardiff Castle
Castle Street   Map Ref **5**
Cardiff CF1 2RB
Tel: 01222 878100   SH

Celtic Manor
The Coldra   Map Ref **6**
Newport NP6 2YA
Tel: 01633 413000   CHH

The Coal Exchange
Mount Stuart Square   Map Ref **7**
Cardiff CF1 6SU
Tel: 01222 452 557   Misc

Conrah Country House Hotel
Chancery   Map Ref **8**
Aberystwyth
Ceredigion SY23 4DF
Tel: 01970 617941   CHH

Court Hotel
Lamphey   Map Ref **9**
Pembrooke SA71 5NT
Tel: 01646 672273   H

Glandwr Manor Hotel
Tresaith   Map Ref **10**
Nr Cardigan
Tel: 01239 810197   H

Gliffaes Country House
Crickhowell   Map Ref **11**
Powys NP8 1RH
Tel: 01874 730371   CHH

Griffin Inn
Llyswen   Map Ref **12**
Brecon LD3 0UR
Tel: 01874 754241   H

Groes Inn
Ty n y Groes   Map Ref **13**
Conway LL32 8TN
Tel: 01492 650545   H

Gwydir Castle
Llanrwst   Map Ref **14**
Gywnedd LL26 0PN
Tel: 01492 641687   SH

Marriott St Pierre Hotel
St Pierre Park   Map Ref **15**
Chepstow NP6 6YA
Tel: 01291 625261   CHH

Min-Y-Mor Hotel
Barmouth   Map Ref **16**
Gwynedd LL42 1HW
Tel: 01341 280555   H

Miskin Manor
Pendoylan Road   Map Ref **17**
Groesfaen
Pontyclun
Mid Glamorgan CF72 8ND
Tel: 01443 224204   CHH

Pale Hall Country House
Pale Estate   Map Ref **18**
Llandderfel
Bala
Gwynedd LL23 7PS
Tel: 01678 530285   H

Penally Abbey
Penally   Map Ref **19**
Nr Tenby
Pembrokeshire SA70 7PY
Tel: 01834 843033   CHH

Portmerrion Hotel
Portmerion LL48 6ET Map Ref **20**
Tel: 01766 770228   H

Richmond Hotel
44-45 Marine Terrace Map Ref **21**
Aberystwyth
Ceredigion SY23 2BX
Tel: 01970 612201   H

St Davids Park Hotel
St Davids Park   Map Ref **22**
Ewloe
Flintshire CH5 3YB
Tel: 01244 520800   CHH

Tredegar House & Park
Newport   Map Ref **23**
South Wales NP1 9YW
Tel: 01633 815880   CHH

West Arms Hotel
Llanarmon Dyffryn   Map Ref **24**
Ceiriog
Ceiriog Valley
Wrexham LL20 7LD
Tel: 01691 600665   H

Ynyshir Hall
Eglwysfach   Map Ref **25**
Machynelleth SY20 8TA
Tel: 01654 781209   H

Region 7 See map on page 137

Adlington Hall
Nr Macclesfield   Map Ref **1**
Cheshire SK10 4LF
Tel: 01625 820 875   SH

Alton Towers Theme Park & Hotel
Alton   Map Ref **2**
Staffordshire ST10 4DB
Tel: 01538 704014   Misc

Appleby Castle
Appleby-in-Westmorland Map Ref **3**
Cumbria CA16 6XH
Tel: 017683 51402   SH

Arley Hall & Gardens
Arley   Map Ref **4**
Northwich
Cheshire CW9 6NA
Tel: 01565 777353   SH

Armathwaite Hall
Bassenthwaite Lake   Map Ref **5**
Keswick
Cumbria CA12 4RE
Tel: 017687 76551   CHH

Astley Hall
Off Hallgate   Map Ref **6**
Astley Park
Chorley
Lancashire PR7 1NP
Tel: 01257 262166   SH

Bramoll Hall
Bramholl Park   Map Ref **7**
Stockport
Cheshire SK7 3NX
Tel: 0161 485 3708   SH

Brantwood
Coniston   Map Ref **8**
Cumbria
Tel: 015394 41396   SH

Calke Abbey
Ticknall   Map Ref **9**
Derby DE73 1LE
Tel: 01332 863822   SH

Capesthorne Hall
Capesthorne   Map Ref **10**
Siddington
Nr Macclesfield
Cheshire SK11 9JY
Tel: 01625 861221   SH

Chester Grosvenor
Eastgate   Map Ref **11**
Chester CH1 1LT
Tel: 01244 324024   H

Chillington Hall
Nr Wolverhampton   Map Ref **12**
Staffordshire WV8 1RE
Tel: 01902 850236   SH

Croxteth Hall & Country Park
Croxteth Hall Lane   Map Ref **13**
Liverpool L12 0HB
Tel: 0151 228 5311   SH

Dalermain
Nr Penrith   Map Ref **14**
Cumbria CA11 0HB
Tel: 017684 86450   SH

De Vere Mottram Hall
Mottram St Andrew   Map Ref **15**
Prestbury
Cheshire SK10 4QT
Tel: 01625 828135   H

Dinham Hall
By the Castle   Map Ref **16**
Ludlow
Shropshire SY8 1EJ
Tel: 01584 876464   H

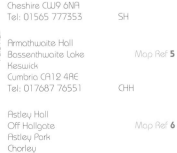

Dorfold Hall
Nantwich   Map Ref **17**
Cheshire CW5 8LD
Tel: 01270 625245   SH

Dunwood Hall
Longsdon   Map Ref **18**
Nr Leek
Staffordshire ST9 9AR
Tel: 01538 385071   SH

Elvaston Castle Country Park & Estate
Museum   Map Ref **19**
Borrowash Road
Elvaston
Derby
Derbyshire DE72 3EP
Tel: 01332 571342   SH

Farlam Hall
Hallbankgate   Map Ref **20**
Brampton
Cumbria CA8 2NG
Tel: 016977 46234   CHH

Farlam Hall

Fischer's at Baslow Hall
Calver Road   Map Ref **21**
Baslow
Derbyshire DE45 1RR
Tel: 01246 583259   CHH

Fischer's at Baslow Hall

Ford Green Hall
Ford Green Road   Map Ref **22**
Smallthorne
Stoke-on-Trent
Staffordshire S76 1NG
Tel: 01782 233195   SH

Frontierland Themepark
Marine Road West   Map Ref **23**
Morecambe Bay
Lancashire LA4 4DG
Tel: 01524 410024   Misc

Gawsworth Hall
Macclesfield   Map Ref **24**
Cheshire
Tel: 01260 223456   SH

Gawthorpe Hall
Padiham   Map Ref **25**
Nr Burnley
Lancashire BB12 8UA
Tel: 01282 770353   SH

Gladstone Working Pottery Museum
Uttoxeter Road   Map Ref **26**
Longton
Stoke-on-Trent
Staffordshire ST3 1PQ
Tel: 01782 319232   Misc

HMS Bronington
Trafford Wharf Road   Map Ref **27**
Trafford Park
Manchester M17 1EX
Tel: 0161 848 8000   Misc

Hawkstone Hall & Gardens
Marchamley   Map Ref **28**
Shrewsbury
Shropshire SY4 5LG
Tel: 01630 685242   SH

Heaton Hall
Prestwich   Map Ref **29**
Manchester
Lancashire M25 2SW
Tel: 0161 773 1231   SH

Hoghton Tower
Nr Preston   Map Ref **30**
Lancashire PR5 0SH
Tel: 01254 852986   SH

Hoole Hall
Warrington Road   Map Ref **31**
Chester
Cheshire CH2 3PD
Tel: 01244 350011   H

Linthwaite House
Bowness-on-Windermere   Map Ref **32**
Cumbria LA23 3JA
Tel: 015394 88600   H

Linthwaite House

Little Moreton Hall
Congleton   Map Ref **33**
Cheshire CW12 4SD
Tel: 01260 272018   SH

Losehill Hall
Peak National Park Centre Map Ref **34**
Derbyshire S30 2WB
Tel: 01433 620373   SH

Merseyside Maritime Museum
Albert Dock   Map Ref **35**
Liverpool L3 4AQ
Tel: 0151 478 4493   Misc

Michaels Nook
Grasmere   Map Ref **36**
Cumbria LA22 9RP
Tel: 015394 35496   CHH

Mickleover Court
Etwall Road   Map Ref **37**
Derby
Derbyshire DE3 8JX
Tel: 01332 521234   H

Mirehouse
Keswick   Map Ref **38**
Cumbria CA12 4QE
Tel: 01768 772287   SH

Mollington Banastre
Parkgate Road   Map Ref **39**
Mollington
Chester CH1 6NN
Tel: 01244 851471   H

Muncaster Castle
Ravenglass   Map Ref **40**
Cumbria CA18 1RQ
Tel: 01229 717614   SH

Naworth Castle
Brampton   Map Ref **41**
Cumbria CA82 2HF
Tel: 016977 3229   SH

The Pavillion Gardens
St Johns Road   Map Ref **42**
Buxton
Derbyshire SK17 6XN
Tel: 01298 23114   SH

The Pheasant Inn
Higher Burwardsley   Map Ref **43**
Tattenhall
Chester CH3 9PF
Tel: 01829 770434   H

Portal Golf & Country Club
Cobblers Cross Lane   Map Ref **44**
Taporley
Cheshire CW6 0DJ
Tel: 01829 733933   H

Riber Hall
Matlock   Map Ref **45**
Derbyshire DE4 5JU
Tel: 01629 582795   CHH

Risley Hall
Derby Road   Map Ref **46**
Risley
Derbyshire DE72 3SS
Tel: 0115 939 9000   SH

Rode Hall
Church Lane   Map Ref **47**
Scholar Green
Cheshire ST7 3QP
Tel: 01270 873237   SH

Rookery Hall Hotel
Worleston   Map Ref **48**
Nantwich
Cheshire CW5 6DQ
Tel: 01270 610016   CHH

Rowton Hall Hotel
Whitchurch Roadon   Map Ref **49**
Chester CH3 6AD
Tel: 01244 335262   H

Royal Northern College of Music
124 Oxford Road   Map Ref **50**
Manchester M13 9RD
Tel: 0161 273 6283   Misc

Shaw Hill Hotel
Whittle-le-Woods   Map Ref **51**
Lancashire PR6 7PP
Tel: 01257 269221   CHH

Shrewsbury Castle & Shropshire Regimental
Museum   Map Ref **52**
Castle Street
Shrewsbury
Shropshire SY1 2RT
Tel: 01743 358516   SH

Shrigley Hall Hotel Golf & Country Club
Pott Shrigley   Map Ref **53**
Macclesfield SK10 5SB
Tel: 01625 575757   CHH

Shugborough Estate
Milford   Map Ref **54**
Stratford
Staffordshire ST18 0QW
Tel: 01889 881388   SH

Tullie House Museum & Art Gallery
Castle Street   Map Ref **55**
Carlisle
Cumbria CA3 8TP
Tel: 01228 34781   Misc

Woolton Redbourne Hotel
Acrefield Road   Map Ref **56**
Woolton
Liverpool L25 5JN
Tel: 0151 421 1500   H

Wordsworth Hotel
Grasmere   Map Ref **57**
Cumbria LA22 9SW
Tel: 015394 35592   CHH

Wordsworth Hotel

Region 8 See map on page 138

42 The Calls
Leeds   Map Ref **1**
West Yorkshire LS2 7EW
Tel: 0113 244 0099   H

Ardsley House Hotel
Doncaster Road   Map Ref **2**
Ardlsey
Barnsley
South Yorkshire S71 5EH
Tel: 01226 309955   H

Aske Hall
Aske   Map Ref **3**
Richmond
North Yorkshire DL10 5HJ
Tel: 01748 850 391   SH

Auckland Castle
Bishop Auckland   Map Ref **4**
Co Durham DL14 7NR
Tel: 01388 6Tel: 01627   SH

Bagden Hall
Wakefield Road   Map Ref **5**
Huddersfield
West Yorkshire HD8 9LE
Tel: 01484 865330   SH

The Bar Convent
17 Blossom Street   Map Ref **6**
York YO2 2AH
Tel: 01904 643238   SH

Bolton Abbey
Skipton   Map Ref **7**
North Yorkshire BD23 6EX
Tel: 01756 710227   SH

Bolton Castle
Leyburn   Map Ref **8**
North Yorkshire DL8 4ET
Tel: 01969 623981   SH

Bradley Court
7-9 Filey Road   Map Ref **9**
Scarborough
North Yorkshire YO11 2SE
Tel: 01723 360 476   H

Captain Cook Birthplace Museum
Stewart Park   Map Ref **10**
Marton
Middlesborough
Cleveland TS7 6AS
Tel: 01642 311 211   Misc

Caythorpe Court
Grantham   Map Ref **11**
Lincolnshire NR32 3EP
Tel: 01400 272521   Misc

Cedar Court Hotel
Denby Dale Road   Map Ref **12**
Wakefield
West Yorkshire WF4 3QZ
Tel: 01924 276310   H

Chillingham Castle & Gardens
Chillingham   Map Ref **13**
Nr Alnwick
Northumberland NE66 5NJ
Tel: 01668 215359   SH

Cliffe Castle
Spring Gardens Lane   Map Ref **14**
Keighley
West Yorkshire BD20 6LH
Tel: 01535 618 230   SH

Crathorne Hall Hotel
Crathorne   Map Ref **15**
Yarm
Teeside TS15 0AR
Tel: 01642 700398   H

De Vere Slaley Hall
Slaley   Map Ref **16**
Hexham
Northumberland NE47 0BY
Tel: 01434 673350   CHH

Slaley Hall

Dissington Hall
Dalton   Map Ref **17**
Ponteland
Northumberland NE18 0AD
Tel: 01661 886063   H

Duncombe Park
Helmsley   Map Ref **18**
Ryedale
York
North Yorkshire YO6 5EB
Tel: 01439 770 213   SH

Fairfax House
Castlegate   Map Ref **19**
York YO1 1RN
Tel: 01904 655543   SH

Grimsthorpe Castle
Grimsthorpe   Map Ref **20**
Bourne
Lincolnshire PE10 0NB
Tel: 01778 591205   SH

Hall Garth Golf & Country Club
Coatham Mundeville   Map Ref **21**
Darlington
Co Durham DL1 3LU
Tel: 01325 300400   CHH

Hellaby Hall Hotel
Old Hellaby Lane   Map Ref **22**
Rotherham
South Yorkshire S66 8SN
Tel: 01709 702701   CHH

Hovingham Hall
Hovingham   Map Ref **23**
North Yorkshire YO6 4LU
Tel: 01653 628206   SH

Kelham Hall
Kelham   Map Ref **24**
Newark
Nottinghamshire NG23 5QX
Tel: 01636 708256   Misc

Linden Hall
Longhorsley   Map Ref **25**
Morpeth
Northumberland NE65 8XF
Tel: 01670 516611   CHH

Lumley Castle
Chester-Le-Street   Map Ref **26**
Co. Durham DH3 4NX
Tel: 0191 389 1111   CHH

Lumley Castle

Middlethorpe Hall
Bishopthorpe Road   Map Ref **27**
York
North Yorkshire YO2 1QB
Tel: 01904 641241   CHH

Millers House Hotel
Middleham   Map Ref **28**
North Yorkshire DL8 4NR
Tel: 01969 622630   CHH

Millers House Hotel

Monk Fryston Hall
Monk Fryston   Map Ref **29**
North Yorkshire LS25 5DU
Tel: 01977 682369   CHH

Mount Royale Hotel
The Mount   Map Ref **30**
York
North Yorkshire YO2 2DA
Tel: 01904 628856   H

National Museum of Photography Film &
Television   Map Ref **31**
Pictureville
Bradford
West Yorkshire BD1 1NQ
Tel: 01274 773399   Misc

National Railway Museum
Leeman Road   Map Ref **32**
York
North Yorkshire YO2 4XJ
Tel: 01904 621261   Misc

Newburgh Priory
Coxwold   Map Ref **33**
York
North Yorkshire YO6 4AS
Tel: 01347 868435   SH

Newby Hall & Gardens
Ripon   Map Ref **34**
North Yorkshire HG4 5AE
Tel: 01423 322583   SH

North York Moors Railway
Pickering Station   Map Ref **35**
Pickering
North Yorkshire YO18 7AJ
Tel: 01751 472508   Misc

Norwood Park
Southwell   Map Ref **36**
Nottinghamshire NG25 0PF
Tel: 01636 815649   SH

Nostell Priory
Nostell   Map Ref **37**
Wakefield
West Yorkshire WF4 1QE
Tel: 01924 864287   Misc

Oulton Hall Hotel
Rothwell Lane   Map Ref **38**
Leeds
West Yorkshire LS26 8HN
Tel: 0113 282 1000   CHH

Ramside Hall Hotel
Carrville   Map Ref **39**
Durham DH1 1TD
Tel: 0191 386 5282   CHH

Redworth Hall Hotel & Country Club
Redworth   Map Ref **40**
Newton Aycliffe
Co. Durham DL5 6NL
Tel: 01388 772442   CHH

Ripley Castle
Ripley Castle Estate Office Map Ref **41**
Harrogate
North Yorkshire HG3 3AY
Tel: 01423 77Tel: 0152   SH

Royal Armouries Museum
Armouries Drive   Map Ref **42**
Leeds
West Yorkshire LS10 1LT
Tel: 0113 220 1999   Misc

Rudding Park House & Hotel
Rudding Park   Map Ref **43**
Follifoot
Harrogate
North Yorkshire HG5 0AU
Tel: 01423 871350   CHH

Sewerby Hall & Gardens
Church Lane   Map Ref **44**
Sewerby
Bridlington YO15 1EA
Tel: 01262 673769   SH

Stoke Rochford Hall
Stoke Rochford   Map Ref **45**
Grantham
Lincolnshire NG33 5EJ
Tel: 01476 530337   SH

Studley Hotel
Swan Road   Map Ref **46**
Harrogate
North Yorkshire HG1 2SE
Tel: 01423 560425   H

Tetleys Brewery Wharf
The Waterfront   Map Ref **47**
Leeds
West Yorkshire LS1 1QG
Tel: 0113 242 0666   Misc

Wentbridge House Hotel
Wentbridge   Map Ref **48**
Nr Pontefract
West Yorkshire WF8 3JJ
Tel: 01977 620444   CHH

Wentbridge House

Worsley Arms Hotel
Hovingham   Map Ref **49**
York YO6 4LA
Tel: 01653 628234   H

Region 9 See map on page 139

Ackergill Tower
By Wick   Map Ref **1**
Caithness KW1 4RG
Tel: 01955 603556   SH

Ackergill Tower

Altamount House Hotel
Blairgowrie   Map Ref **2**
Perthshire PH10 6JN
Tel: 01250 873512   H

Ardoe House Hotel
Blairs   Map Ref **3**
South deeside Road
Aberdeen AB12 5YP
Tel: 01224 867355   H

Ardoe House Hotel

Ardsheal House
Kentallen Of Appin   Map Ref **4**
Argyll PA38 4BX
Tel: 01631 740227   H

Atholl Palace
Pitlochry   Map Ref **5**
Perthshire PH16 5LY
Tel: 01796 472400   SH

Auchen Castle Hotel
Beattock   Map Ref **6**
Dumfries & Galloway DG10 9SH
Tel: 01683 300407   CHH

Auchrannie Country House Hotel
Auchrannie Road   Map Ref **7**
Isle of Arran KA27 8BZ
Tel: 01770 302234   CHH

Auchterarder House
Auchterarder   Map Ref **8**
Perthshire PH3 1DZ
Tel: 01764 663646   CHH

Ayton Castle
Eyemouth   Map Ref **9**
Berwickshire TD14 5RD
Tel: 018907 81212   SH

Balbirnie House
Balbirnie Park   Map Ref **10**
Markinch
Fife KY7 6NE
Tel: 01592 610066   CHH

Ballathie House Hotel
Nr Perth   Map Ref **11**
Perthshire PH1 4QN
Tel: 01250 883268   CHH

Balnain House
40 Huntly Street   Map Ref **12**
Inverness
Inverness-shire IV3 5HR
Tel: 01463 715757   H

Bowhill
Selkirk   Map Ref **13**
Borders TD7 5ET
Tel: 01750 22204   SH

Braemar Castle
Braemar   Map Ref **14**
Grampian AB35 5XR
Tel: 013397 41219   SH

Bunchrew House Hotel
Brunchrew   Map Ref **15**
Inverness IV3 6TA
Tel: 01463 234917   H

Callendar House
Callendar Park   Map Ref **16**
Falkirk FK1 1YR
Tel: 01324 503770   CHH

Carnegie Club at Skibo Castle
Dornoch   Map Ref **17**
Sutherland IV25 3RQ
Tel: 01862 894600   CHH

Skibo Castle

Castleton House Hotel
Castleton of Eassie   Map Ref **18**
Glamis
Angus DD8 1SJ
Tel: 01307 840340   CHH

Conchra House Hotel
Sallachy Road   Map Ref **19**
Ardelve
Kyle of Lochalsh
Ross-shire IV40 8DZ
Tel: 01599 555233   CHH

Coul House Hotel
Contin   Map Ref **20**
By Strathpeffer
Ross-shire IV14 9EY
Tel: 01997 421945   CHH

Craigmonie Hotel
Annfield Road   Map Ref **21**
Inverness IV2 3HX
Tel: 01463 231649   H

Cringletie House Hotel
Peebles EH45 8PL   Map Ref **22**
Tel: 01721 730233   CHH

Cromlix House
Kinbuck   Map Ref **23**
Nr Dunblane
Perthshire FK15 9JT
Tel: 01786 822125   CHH

Culloden House Hotel
Inverness   Map Ref **24**
Inverness-shire IV1 2NZ
Tel: 01463 790461   CHH

Dalmeny House
South Queensferry   Map Ref **25**
Edinburgh EH30 9TQ
Tel: 0131 3311888   SH

Dalmunzie House
Spittal O'Glenshee   Map Ref **26**
Blairgowrie
Perthshire PH10 7QG
Tel: 01250 885224   CHH

Dornoch Castle
Castle Street   Map Ref **27**
Dornoch
Sutherland IV25 3SD
Tel: 01862 810216   H

Dunrobin Castle
Dunrobin   Map Ref **28**
Golspie
Sutherland KW10 6SF
Tel: 01408 633177   SH

Fairburn
Marybank   Map Ref **29**
Muir of Ord
Ross-shire IV6 7RT
Tel: 01997 433397   Misc

Fasque
Fettercairn   Map Ref **30**
Laurencekirk
Kincardineshire AB30 1DN
Tel: 01561 340202   SH

Floors Castle
Kelso TD5 7SF   Map Ref **31**
Tel: 01573 223333   SH

Floors Castle

Fort Augustus Abbey
Fort Augustus   Map Ref **32**
Inverness-shire PH32 4BD
Tel: 01320 366233   Misc

Glamis Castle
Glamis   Map Ref **33**
By Forfar
Angus DD8 1RJ
Tel: 01307 840393   SH

Glen Mhor Hotel
9 - 12 Ness Bank   Map Ref **34**
Inverness IV2 4SG
Tel: 01463 234308   H

Glenfarg Hotel
Glenfarg   Map Ref **35**
Nr Kinross
Perthshire PH12 9NU
Tel: 01577 830241   H

Glenfarg Hotel

Glenturret Distillery
Crieff   Map Ref **36**
Perthshire PH7 4HA
Tel: 01764 656565   Misc

Hopetoun House
South Queensferry   Map Ref **37**
West Lothian EH30 9SL
Tel: 0131 331 2451   H

Inver Lodge Hotel
Lochinver   Map Ref **38**
Sutherland IV27 4LU
Tel: 01571 844496   H

Inverlochy Castle
Torlundy   Map Ref **39**
Fort William
Inverness-shire PH33 6SN
Tel: 01397 702177   CHH

Johnstounburn House
Humbie   Map Ref **40**
Nr Edinburgh
East Lothian EH36 5PL
Tel: 01875 833696   CHH

Johnstonburn House

Kelburn Castle
Fairlie   Map Ref **41**
Ayrshire KA29 0BE
Tel: 01475 568685   SH

Kinfauns Castle
Nr Perth PH2 7JZ   Map Ref **42**
Tel: 01738 620777   CHH

Kinveachy Lodge
The Strathspey Estate Office
Heathfield   Map Ref **43**
Grantown on Spey
Moray PH26 3LG
Tel: 01479 872529   Misc

Lands of Loyal Hotel
Alyth   Map Ref **44**
Perthshire PH11 8JQ
Tel: 01828 633151   H

Letham Grange Hotel
Colliston   Map Ref **45**
Angus DD11 4RL
Tel: 01241 890373   CHH

Loch Melfort
Arduaine   Map Ref **46**
By Oban
Argyll PA34 4XG
Tel: 01852 200233   H

Loch Torridon Hotel
Achnasheen   Map Ref **47**
Ross-shire IV22 2EY
Tel: 01445 791242   CHH

Lovat Arms Hotel
Beauly   Map Ref **48**
Nr Inverness IV4 7BS
Tel: 01463 782313   H

Montgreenan Mansion House Hotel
Montgreenan Estate   Map Ref **49**
Kilwinning
Ayrshire KA13 7QZ
Tel: 01294 557733   CHH

Montgreenan Mansion House

Murrayshall Country House
Scone   Map Ref **50**
Perthshire PH2 7PH
Tel: 01738 551171   CHH

Nivingston Country House
Cleish Hills   Map Ref **51**
Nr Kinross
Kinross-shire KY13 7LS
Tel: 01577 850216   CHH

Piersland House Hotel
Craigend Road   Map Ref **52**
Troon
Ayrshire KA10 6HD
Tel: 01292 314747   H

Roman Camp Countrry House Hotel
Callander   Map Ref **53**
Perthshire
Tel: 01877 330003   CHH

Rothiemurchus Estate
Drumintoul Lodge   Map Ref **54**
By Aviemore
Inverness-shire PH22 1QH
Tel: 01479 810858   Misc

Roxburgh Hotel & Golf Course
Kelso   Map Ref **55**
Roxburghshire TD5 8JZ
Tel: 01573 450331   CHH

Royal Botanic Garden Edinburgh
20A Inverleith Row   Map Ref **56**
Edinburgh
Midlothian EH3 5LR
Tel: 0131 552 7171   Misc

Royal Museum of Scotland
Chambers Street   Map Ref **57**
Edinburgh EH1 1JF
Tel: 0131 247 4206   Misc

Royal Scottish Academy of Music & Drama
100 Renfrew Street   Map Ref **58**
Glasgow G2 3DB
Tel: 0141 332 4101   Misc

Scone Palace
Perth   Map Ref **59**
Perthshire PH2 6BD
Tel: 01738 552300   SH

Scotch Whisky Heritage Centre
354 Castlehill   Map Ref **60**
The Royal Mile
Edinburgh EH1 2NE
Tel: 0131 220 0441   Misc

Summer Isles
Achiltibuie   Map Ref **61**
Ross-Shire IV26 2YG
Tel: 01854 622282   H

Taychreggan
Kilchrenan   Map Ref **62**
By Taynuilt
Argyll PA35 1HQ
Tel: 01866 833211   H

Tulloch Castle Hotel
Tulloch Castle Drive   Map Ref **63**
Dingwall
Ross-shire IV15 9ND
Tel: 01349 861325   CHH

Uig Hotel
Uig   Map Ref **64**
Isle of Skye IV51 9YE
Tel: 01470 542205   H

Westerwood Hotel Golf & Country Club
St. Andrews Drive   Map Ref **65**
Cumbernauld
Glasgow G68 0EW
Tel: 01236 457171   CHH

The Aftermath

Acknowledgements

The idea for this book arose during the course of a conversation between Eddie Hoare of Elegant Days and Julian West of Kensington West Productions. Eddie does a lot of entertaining at sporting events, and Julian, who is a publisher, likes to be entertained. They both like to party, and clearly thought this was a good enough reason for putting together a book on the subject. Planning the Perfect Party is the result.

Clearly then we owe a debt of gratitude to Elegant Days without whom Planning the Perfect Party would not have been possible. Their knowledge of the entertainment/hospitality industry is second to none, and their enthusiasm is contagious. Eddie Hoare and his colleagues have been willing - no, eager - to help in every possible way.

We are also grateful to all our contributors, each an expert in their chosen field, who have written such informative and amusing articles without reward and at quite short notice sometimes. Equally, we appreciate all the photographs which so many people have kindly provided to illustrate the ideas put forward in Planning the Perfect Party.

To all at Kensington West Productions - thanks! Thanks also to you, dear reader, for buying the book.

And finally - use Planning the Perfect Party to to just that - plan a party, hold a party and enjoy the party!

courtesy of Dennis Ramsey

1st Leisure Supplies
Leisure House
89 Seabourne Road
Southbourne
Bournemouth BH5 2HF
Tel: 01202 429 829

A1 Yacht Charter
Southampton Road
Paulsgrove
Portsmouth PO6 4RJ
Tel: 01705 210 277

Ackergill Tower
By Wick
Caithness
Scotland KW1 4RG
Tel: 01955 603556

The Admirable Crichton
6 Camberwell Trading Estate
Denmark Road
London SE5 9LB
Tel: 0171 733 8113

Balloons To Go
160 Eardley Road
London SW16 5TG
Tel: 0181 679 7766

Banana Split
11 Carlisle Road
London NW9 0HD
Tel: 0181 200 1234

Bentley Wildfowl & Motor Museum
Halland
Lewes
East Sussex BN8 5AF
Tel: 01825 840 573

By Word of Mouth
22 Glenville Mews
Kimber Road
London
SW18 4NJ
Tel: 0181 871 9566

Carnegie Club at Skibo Castle
Dornoch Sutherland
Scotland IV25 3RQ
Tel: 01862 894 600

The Carnegie Club
64-66 Bury Walk
London SW3 6QB
Tel: 0171 351 4321

Chimneys Restaurant
Hall Street
Long Melford
Sudbury
Suffolk CO10 0JR
Tel: 01787 379 806

Classic Lighting
Little Bramshot Farm
Cove Road
Fleet
Hampshire GU13 8RT
Tel: 01252 860 330

Classic Wings
The Aerodrome
Clacton-on-Sea
Essex CO15 1AG
Tel: 01255 473 832

Creative Breaks
364-366 Fulham Road
London SW10 9UU
Tel: 0171 795 0155

The Creative Catering Company
Vekk House
Near Winchester
Hampshire SO21 1EG
Tel: 01962 779 792

Danco Plc
The Pavilion Centre
Frog Lane
Coalpit Heath
Bristol BS36 2NW
Tel: 01454 250 222

Davidoff Distribution UK Ltd
1 Tillingbourne Court
Dorking Business Park
Dorking
Surrey RH4 17J
Tel: 01306 882 411

Dennis Ramsey
37b New Cavendish Street
London W1M 8JR
Tel: 0171 486 5353

Elegant Days
The Lodge
Hatton House
Hatton
Warwickshire CV35 7LD
Tel: 01926 842 044

Elegant Days (Enterprises) Ltd
60 Maltings Place
Bagleys Lane
London SW6 2BX
Tel: 0171 736 7772

courtesy of Searcy's & Joanna Plumbe Photography

Elements Entertainments Agency
127 Bath Road
Old Town
Swindon SN1 4AX
Tel: 01793 431 543

Expo Flora Ltd
"The Chestnuts"
29 Warwick Road
Wellesbourne
Warwickshire CV35 9NA
Tel: 01789 470 847

FACE The Face Painting Association
42 Nuffield Drive
Droitwich
Worcestershire WR9 0DJ
Tel: 01905 779 884

Fanfare 3000
The Folly
Pinner Hill Road
Pinner
Middlesex HA5 3YQ
Tel: 0181 429 3000

Farlam Hall Country House Hotel
Brampton
Cumbria CA8 2NG
Tel: 016977 46234

Fisher Lighting
Falcon Wharf
Lombard Road
London SW11 3RF
Tel: 0171 8Tel: 01 4100

Flowers Unlimited
The Courtyard
Newbrough
Hexham NE47 5AT
Tel: 01434 674 443

Freddie Maynell At Searcy's
124 Bolingbroke Road
London SW11 1DA
Tel: 0589 751 346

Freedom
FHQ
38 Naylor Road
Whetstone
London N20 0HN
Tel: 0181 445 8687

Gilmour & Pether
Unit 4
Borough Road
Buckingham Road Industrial Estate
Brackley
Northants NN13 7BE
Tel: 01280 701 611

Gorgeous Gourmets
Gresham Way
Wimbledon
London SW19 8ED
Tel: 0181 944 7771

Grimsthorpe & Drummond Castle Trust Limited
Grimsthorpe Estate Office
Bourne
Lincolnshire PE10 0NB
Tel: 01778 591 205

The Ice Box
Unti A35/36
New Covent Garden Market
London SW8 5EE
Tel: 0171 498 0800

Irvin Leisure Ltd
Victoria House
Main Street
Hanworth
Middlesex TW13 6SU
Tel: 0181 893 8993

Kingston PR
4 Reeds Park
Ufton
Leamington Spa
Warwickshire CV33 9PR
Tel: 01926 614 696

Linda's Pantry
Unit E3
Hilton Business Centre
East Wittering
West Sussex PO20 8RL
Tel: 01243 671 200

The London Gin Company
8 Windward House
Plantation Wharf
London SW11 3TU
Tel: 0171 223 5723

Lucas Lloyd Marketing
63 Astrop Road
Kings Sutton
Banbury OX17 3PS
Tel: 01295 811 130

The Marquee Hire Company
The Coach House
Yelvertoft
Northamptonshire NN6 6LX
Tel: 01788 822 922

Masquerade
63 Crown Road
Barkingside
Ilford
Essex IG6 1NN
Tel: 0181 551 4635

MUTA
42 Heath Street
Tamworth
Staffordshire B79 7JH
Tel: 01827 52337

Oddbins
31-33 Weir Road
Wimbledon
London SW19 8UG
Tel: 0181 944 4400

Owen Brown Ltd
Station Road
Castle Donnington
Derbyshire DE74 2NL
Tel: 01332 850 000

Pains Fireworks Ltd
Bretby Business Park
Ashby Road
Stanhope Bretby
Nr Barton on Trent DE15 0YZ
Tel: 01283 553 141

Party Pieces
1438 Wimborne Road
Kinson
Bournemouth BH10 7AF
Tel: 01202 590 890

Peeks the Event Makers
Reid Street
Christchurch BH23 2BT
Tel: 01202 489 489

Joanna Plumbe Photography
43 Muncaster Road
London SW11 6NX
Tel: 0171 978 4814

Russell Twining Bere Ltd
Exhibition Nurseries
Main Street
Mursley
Milton Keynes MK17 0RT
Tel: 01296 720 006

S & D Leisure
1 Chadwicks Depot
Collingham Street
Cheetham Hall
Manchester M8 8RQ
Tel: 0161 835 2758

The Savoy
1 Savoy Hill
London WC2R 0BP
Tel: 0171 836 4343

The Science Museum
Exhibition Road
London SW7 2DD
Tel: 0171 938 8184

Searcy's
124 Bolingbroke Grove
London SW11 1DA
Tel: 0171 585 0505

Sellers ArenaScene Ltd
International House
Chapel Hill
Huddersfield HD1 3EE
Tel: 01484 435 569

Spicers of Hythe
The Hamperage
Unit S2, Lympne Business Park
Hythe
Kent CT21 4LR
Tel: 01303 262 398

Theme Traders
The Stadium
Oaklands Road
London NW2 6DL
Tel: 0181 452 8518

Twizzle Entertainment
Chantry House
4 Umbria Street
Putney
London SW15 5DP
Tel: 0374 606 814

Virgin Balloon Flights Ltd
Unit 1
Stafford Park 12
Telford
Shropshire TF3 3BJ
Tel: 0990 228 483

Water Sculptures Ltd
St George's Studios
St George's Quay
Lancaster LA1 5QJ
Tel: 01524 64430

Weston Park
Weston-under-Lizard
Nr Shifnal
Shropshire TF11 8LE
Tel: 01952 850 201

William Bartholomew Party Organising Ltd
18 The Talina Centre
Bagleys Lane
London SW6 2BW
Tel: 0171 731 8328

Woods River Cruises
PO Box 177
London SE3 9JA
Tel: 0171 481 2711

courtesy of Searcy's & Joanna Plumbe Photography

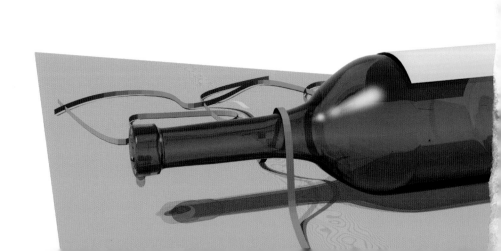